BRITAIN

IN OLD PHOTOGRAPHS

WEST BROMWICH

PEOPLE & PLACES

TERRY PRICE

SUTTON PUBLISHING

Christmas 2003
With Love
from
Helena xx

Sutton Publishing Limited
Phoenix Mill · Thrupp · Stroud
Gloucestershire · GL5 2BU

First published 2003

Reprinted 2003

Title page photograph: An early twentieth-century
view of Dartmouth Square in the steam-tram era.
Note the absence of tram standards which were
erected in 1903 during electrification of the system.
The bakery premises of Sydney Perry at 148 High
Street (left) were taken over by Joseph Broadhead in
1910. (*T.J.H. Price*)

British Library Cataloguing in Publication Data
A catalogue record for this book is available from the
British Library.

ISBN 0-7509-3678-9

Typeset in 10.5/13.5 Photina.
Typesetting and origination by
Sutton Publishing Limited.
Printed and bound in England by
J.H. Haynes & Co. Ltd, Sparkford.

Other books by the author
Great Bridge & District • Great Bridge Revisited
Great Bridge Memories (2004)

Probably the best-known character in the town centre during the 1940s, '50s and '60s was Lionel Peel
who, from his invalid carriage, sold newspapers on Dartmouth Square. Pictured here with Horace Jukes in
about 1966 outside Broadhead's the bakers, Lionel is fondly remembered for his cheerful disposition and
reliability in all weathers. (*T.J.H. Price*)

CONTENTS

A Birmingham Corporation brush-bodied bogie tramcar operating on the short-working No. 73 route between Birmingham and Carters Green waits outside the Tower Cinema on 9 August 1938. The film being advertised in the background is *The Buccaneer* starring Fredric March and Akim Tamiroff. (*National Tramway Museum*)

Alderman Reuben Farley JP, 1826–99.
The first and five-times Mayor of West Bromwich.

INTRODUCTION

West Bromwich as a place of habitation was founded in Saxon times and for many years was purely an agricultural community. The use of two Anglo-Saxon words 'Broom' and 'Wic' give us a clue to its early beginnings. The broom plant with its yellow flowers grew in great profusion on the heathlands of the district, while 'wic' was a Saxon name meaning village or place. Over the centuries the spelling of the name 'Broomwic' gradually evolved to become Bromwich, with 'West' being added sometime around the fourteenth century to distinguish it from Castle Bromwich, and Little Bromwich. For a long time it was thought that West Bromwich was not included in the Domesday Book of 1086 until it was discovered that, through a clerical error, it had been inserted into the Northampton section along with other manors held by William Fitz-Ansculph, Baron of Dudley.

The population at this time was somewhere around sixty, rising to only 5,687 at the time of the first national census in 1801. This coincided with the introduction of the Enclosure Act, which resulted in parcels of common or wasteland being allocated to all freeholders. In West Bromwich the most extensive common was called Bromwich Heath, which stretched from Sandwell Road eastwards to where Trinity Way crosses the High Street, and southwards from Mayers Green to Barton Street post office at the top of Bromford Lane. The heath was traversed by the Turnpike Road, along which stagecoaches from London to Holyhead used to run. This was the area that was later to become the main business and shopping centre of the town, including of course the famous 'Golden Mile'.

It is interesting to note that for three-quarters of its perimeter West Bromwich had the River Tame for its boundary and a traveller entering the town from any direction, except from the east, would have to cross over it.

The Balls Hill branch of the Birmingham Canal opened from Spon Lane to Wednesbury via Golds Hill in 1769, making the sight of a string of packhorses laden with coal coming up Holloway Bank a thing of the past. The first railway station in the locality opened in 1837 on the north side of Newton Road, but was superseded in 1863 by a new one which for a few months was called 'West Bromwich'. It was not until 1854 that the railway reached the centre of the town. In that year the Birmingham, Wolverhampton and Dudley Railway was opened with a station located off Paradise Street. A horse-drawn tram service, between Hockley and Dudley Port, and Carters Green to Hill Top, was opened to the public on Whit Monday 20 May 1872. Steam trams, which were introduced in 1883, continued until 1902 when West Bromwich Corporation decided to take over the system and proceed with electrification. On Sunday 2 April 1939 double-decker buses replaced these trams by taking over the main route to Birmingham.

West Bromwich has been the birthplace of several well-known commodities which became household names. The Revd John Hudson, who began his ministry at Mayers Green Chapel in 1801, had a son, Robert Spear Hudson, the inventor of the first soap powder ever to be made. It was called 'Hudsons Dry Soap', and the multi-storey car park on West Bromwich Ringway now occupies the site of the works. After the First World War, Lever Bros, the manufacturers of Sunlight Soap, took over the firm and closed down the

West Bromwich works. The memory of this world famous soap powder lived on for a while in the form of Hudson's Passage in the High Street, which unfortunately no longer exists, a retail outlet having recently been built over it.

Corrugated sheeting was another item invented in West Bromwich, by John Spencer, proprietor of the Phoenix Iron Foundry in Ryders Green at the end of Phoenix Street, which incidentally takes its name from the works. One day in 1844 a sheet of iron, placed as a guard against the side of a rolling machine, fell into the rollers while they were in motion. The crumpled sheet was thrown aside, but later John Spencer noticed that the resultant bends had made it stronger. He took out a patent under the name of 'Currugated Iron' but left the manufacturing to others.

The firm of George Salter & Co. Ltd had its beginnings in 1760 within a small cottage in Bilston, where, it is believed, the first spring balance was made. It was an instrument of 16oz capacity, known in those days as a pocket steelyard. Manufacture of springs on a large scale commenced in West Bromwich about 1790 on a site now occupied by the Howard Johnson Hotel, and during the nineteenth century the range of products was considerably extended. The production of spring balances was at the same time developed, both in types and quantities, and Salter weighing machines began to be used across the world.

The development of West Bromwich into a modern and progressive town during the late nineteenth century can, in the main, be attributed to the tireless energy and zeal of one man, Reuben Farley. No individual before or since has contributed so much to the welfare of his fellow man through either public service or as a great benefactor. As Guardian of the Poor, a title held for fourteen years, he showed an abiding concern for the working class, who liked and admired him enormously. Reuben Farley was born at 146 Whitehall Road, Great Bridge, on 27 January 1826 to parents Elizabeth and Thomas Farley, his father being a mining engineer. In his youth and early manhood he availed himself of every opportunity for learning and self-improvement open to him. In those days there was a Mechanics Institute opposite Wesley Chapel in the High Street where young Reuben became a diligent student, and in after-years ascribed his success to the training he received there. At the age of twenty-one he entered business on his own account as a coal master, and together with his brother-in-law, George Taylor, purchased the Summit Foundry near Spon Lane. He afterwards became Chairman of Fellows, Moreton & Clayton Ltd, the largest canal carriers in the country, and was also Chairman of Edwin Danks Ltd, boiler manufacturers, of Oldbury. Later he became a Director of the Hamstead Colliery Co., and had a large interest in the Sandwell Park Colliery Company as well. Reuben then secured a seat on the council and, when the town was incorporated in 1882, was chosen as the first mayor. He went on to serve a further four terms after which time he had the distinction of being made the first Freeman of West Bromwich. In 1897 a magnificent clock tower was erected by public subscription at Carters Green in his honour. He died on 11 March 1899 at the age of seventy-three.

In conclusion, I hope that the pictures contained within these pages will be a nostalgic reminder of not only the changes in buildings and streets that have occurred during the last century, but also of the community spirit which existed in those far off halcyon days when West Bromwich truly was the premier town of the Midlands.

Terence J.H. Price, July 2003

Chapter One

The Town Centre, Lyng & Spon Lane

Dartmouth Square, *c.* 1965. Through traffic along the High Street to this part of the town ceased during the early 1970s as a result of redevelopment and pedestrianisation of the area. One of this square's more unusual features was the underground lavatories, the gentlemen's entrance being just visible next to the clock on the left of the picture. (*Anthony Page*)

Looking down the High Street from Dartmouth Square, *c.* 1905. The tram standards supporting electric overhead cables, centre of the picture, were moved to the pavement edges in about 1914 in order to create more space on the highway for other vehicles. The drinking fountain on the left was erected in 1885 by Reuben Farley in memory of his mother Elizabeth. (*T.J.H. Price*)

A similar view of Dartmouth Square some fifteen years later, in 1920. Open-top trams, like the one seen leaning alarmingly to one side, had their upper decks enclosed in 1924 when Birmingham Corporation took over the routes. Note that the central tram standards have gone, with a clock replacing the fountain which had been relocated to Dartmouth Park in 1911. (*T.J.H. Price*)

The Bull's Head, nicknamed 'The Wrexham', 146 High Street, March 1961. Before these premises were built in 1835, the eighteenth-century Boot Inn, also known as the 'Bull's Head', was located on the opposite side of Spon Lane (right). In 1834 the Dartmouth Hotel (formerly the Dartmouth Arms) was built on the site. (*Sidney Darby*)

The Spring Balance public house, photographed here on 3 August 1968 with Cyril Edgar Gibson as landlord, was originally called 'The Stores'. Its new name, effective from 20 November 1962, was apparently chosen because of the pub's proximity to the premises of spring manufacturer George Salter & Co. Ltd. Christine Osborne was licensee when this hostelry closed on 28 January 1979. The Midland Bank next door was vacated soon afterwards in 1986. (*Alan Price*)

Martin Dunn's employees' excursion, 19 June 1926, pictured outside their premises at 142 High Street, next to the Fox & Dogs pub. Established in 1861, this firm of plate and sheet glass merchants specialised in all types of glass for the building, shopfitting and the engineering trade. When the business closed after trading for over one hundred years the building became a garment factory. (*T.J.H. Price*)

The Steam Packet (Puffing Billy), 47 Spon Lane, 13 July 1968, when John Harvey Baker was the landlord. One of twenty-two pubs in Spon Lane, these premises closed on 28 March 1971 with Michael Stuart Edmunds on record as the last licensee. Also in the picture is Stan Willetts' electrical shop, established in 1947 and now trading from new premises in Queens Square. (*Alan Price*)

The Plough, 40 Overend Street pictured on 11 May 1961, when Francis Arthur Bradley was licensee. The pub was remarkable in having very few changes of licensees throughout its life, John Reeves and Sydney Joseph Twist being noted for their longevity during the first half of the twentieth century. Frederick Daulman was the landlord when it closed on 31 August 1975. (*Andrew Maxam*)

Dart Social, champions of the Spon Lane Domino League (north section) 1967, celebrating their success at the Dart Spring Social Club, Overend Street. In 1961, Jack and Beattie Thompson, pictured fourth and fifth from the left, were appointed the club's stewards, Jack serving fifteen years until his death in 1976 and Beattie a further six years until closure of the premises in 1982. (*Beattie Thompson*)

Trinity Road, looking towards upper High Street, *c.* 1910, with the old Central Police Station just visible in the centre. In 1973 the police station, along with all of the properties on the left, was demolished in order to construct Trinity Way dual carriageway. As a result the houses on the right are now served by a separate walkway. (*Andrew Maxam*)

The Church Tavern, 87 Trinity Road. When this picture was taken in about 1965, Josephine May Espley was in residence, having been the licensee from 2 January 1958. She was still the landlady when it closed on 16 June 1968. This row of buildings, including the pub, was demolished soon afterwards when the present-day Trinity Way was constructed. (*Andrew Maxam*)

Upper High Street, *c.* 1915. An open-top South Staffordshire tramcar heading towards Birmingham has just passed the Lewisham Hotel on the right, where William Arthur Price was the licensee. Thynne Street on the right has the Thynne Stores off-licence on its corner; a later occupant of these premises was Victoria Wine Co. (*T.J.H. Price*)

Thynne Street, *c.* 1910, looking towards Beeches Road where at 568 feet it becomes the highest point in West Bromwich. Sela the Traditional Sweet Company founded in 1882 by Arthur and Elizabeth Roberts is presently based here. (*T.J.H. Price*)

A view of Herbert Street with the Beeches Road entrance to Dartmouth Park in the distance, *c*. 1910. It was in this street at No. 32 that Hollywood actress Madeleine Carroll was born to parents Helene and John Carroll in 1906. Herbert Street was described as 'new' in 1869, with most of the houses being built during the following thirteen years. (*T.J.H. Price*)

Beeches Road was constructed between 1867 and 1885 from plans submitted to the highway committee by George B. Nicholls, a West Bromwich architect and surveyor. It followed the line of an ancient horse road described in 1776 as leading from Mayers Green towards the Three Mile Oak Turnpike. Today only the first six houses on the left of this picture, dating from around 1910, remain as a result of the Trinity Way/Expressway interchange cutting across here. (*Ken Rock*)

This picture shows the Birmingham Road around 1910 where it passes Bagnall Street (left) and Roebuck Lane (right). In September 1834 James Doughty commenced a horse-bus service from Birmingham to West Bromwich along this road. On 20 June 1836 Mark Robinson became the first fatality when he fell from one of Doughty's buses near the Three Mile Oak. (*T.J.H. Price*)

Beeches Road Methodist Church, Sunday School Anniversary, 1951. Back row, left to right: David Rivers, Brian Hamilton, Revd David Matthews, John Hall. Fifth row: Tom Rivers, Frank Rivers, Maggie Barber, Pat Simmons, -?-. Fourth row: Len Pritchard, -?-, Ivy Janney, Pat Bourne, Betty Holland, -?-, Pauline Turford, Margaret Holland, Jean Law, -?-, Janet Howman, Mary Quance, -?-, -?-, Jean Maybury, Edna Quance. Third row: Bill Jeavons, ? Hickman, John Quance, Robert Quance. Second row: Muriel ?, Valerie Hazel, Evelyn Matthews, Valerie Bourne, -?-, Francis ?, Olive ?, Diane Hickman, Heather Lovett, -?-, Pat Hazel, ? Jeavons, Barry Lovett, -?-, -?-, -?-, Alan Hamilton. (*Evelyn Gough*)

Len Millard, captain of West Bromwich Albion, holds the FA Cup aloft after the team had defeated Preston North End 3–2 in the final at Wembley on Saturday 1 May 1954 in front of 99,852 fans. From left to right: Jimmy Dudley, Frank Griffin, Jimmy Dugdale, Len Millard, Joe Kennedy, Reg 'Paddy' Ryan, Ray Barlow. (*Win Moore*)

One of West Bromwich Albion's greatest players, Jesse Pennington, visits The Hawthorns on Saturday 19 August 1953. West Bromwich-born Jesse not only captained England but also the 'Baggies', leading them to the First Division Championship in 1920 with a record-breaking 60 points and 104 goals. Left to right: Vic Buckingham (manager), Johnny Nicholls, Jesse Pennington, Ken Hodgkisson. (*Ken Hodgkisson*)

Holloway United FC, *c.* 1960. Alf Broadbent (back row, second from right) was in later years the recipient of an award from league officials recognising his thirty-year playing career within the West Bromwich Sunday League. Back row, left to right: David Martin, -? -, -?-, Dennis ?, -?-, -?-, Alf Broadbent, -?-. Front row: -?-, Billy Hughes, -?-, Tony Birch, Roy Bennington. (*Billy Hughes*)

A VE Day party in Roebuck Street, 8 May 1945. Seated behind the table in the foreground, third and fourth from right are: Pat Hazel and Valerie Hazel. Front row, first, second, third and fourth from right: Pat Bourne, Valerie Bourne, Evelyn Matthews and Betty Holland. Among those at the back: Murray Matthews, Sadie Davies and Florence 'Topsey' Hazel. (*Evelyn Gough*)

Ye Olde Bell Inn, 108 Spon Lane, when Eric Higginson was landlord, 11 May 1961. This Darby's pub, located between George Street and Boulton Road, had Harry Whittingham as the licensee when it closed on 2 November 1975. (*Andrew Maxam*)

The annual Maypole Festival at the Church of the Good Shepherd, Spon Lane, *c.* 1939. Back row, left to right: -?-, Jesse Orbell, Kathy Neenan, -?-, -?-, Billy Evans, Jim Ward, -?-, Pat Neenan, Edith Haywood, Ann Phipps, -?-, -?-, Marion Bodley, -?-, Ray Ward, Teddy Groom, -?-, Eric Neenan. Third row: Doreen Jenkins, Edith Evans, -?-, Margaret Bate, Peter Bate, John Rock, Muriel Orbell (May Queen). Among those in the second row: Mary Phipps, Beatrice Rock, Elsie Orbell, Joan Rock. (*Elsie Cartwright*)

The Anchor Inn ('Ma' Fletcher's) 160 Spon Lane, 6 March 1965. This hostelry was situated between Boulton Road and Francis Street, Hugh Livingstone Gilliand being the licensee. One of the longest serving licensees was Mary Ann Fletcher who from 1930 managed the pub for over twenty-five years. Landlord Michael Steward Edmunds closed the doors for the last time on 1 February 1970. (*Andrew Maxam*)

The Good Shepherd Church with St John concert party, *c.* 1968. Back row, left to right: Michael Steele, Derek Woodyatt, Revd Frank Powell, Stan Woodyatt, Len Fancote. Middle row: Jim Baggott, Alice Collett, ? Powell, Jean Walters, Nellie Fancote, Ivy Woodyatt, Doris Collett, Frank Collett, Betty Welch, Mike Carroll. Front row: Hilary Powell, Christine Richardson, -?-, Helen Powell, Elizabeth Powell, -?-, -?-, -?-. (*Ian Collett*)

Hannah Dorothy Mortiboys stands on the doorstep of Walter Clarence Mortiboys' confectionery shop in Spon Lane, *c.* 1926. Note the diamond board on the right advertising 'Monster Minerals' at 1*d* and 3*d* a bottle. When the shop closed around 1934 Walter and his family moved to 192 Phoenix Street, where he set up in business repairing boots and shoes. (*Margaret Mortiboys*)

The White Swan, 334 Spon Lane, also known as 'The Manchester', *c.* 1938. When this picture was taken Sarah Elizabeth Grigg had been the licensee for eight years. She was afterwards succeeded by Samuel Smith. During the 1950s and '60s the pub was well known as a popular venue for jazz bands and their followers. (*Keith Hodgkins*)

The Stour Valley Tavern, 227 Spon Lane, on the corner of Grice Street, 18 May 1948. Mitchells & Butlers took over this property from Cheshire's Windmill Brewery in 1913 with Harry Crees as the landlord, and indeed when this photograph was taken thirty-five years later another member of the Crees family, Mary, was licensee. It closed in 1973. (*Andrew Maxam*)

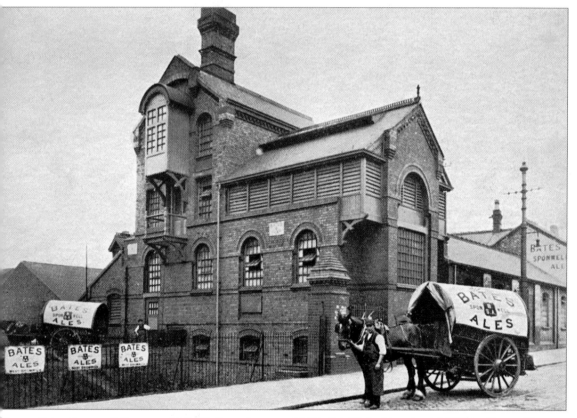

Henry Bates Sponwell Brewery, 119–21 Spon Lane, *c.* 1910. Established in about 1880 by Henry Thomas Bates, the brewery was situated on the corner of Sams Lane until approximately 1922, when production appears to have ceased. The property eventually became Spon Lane Service Station and in 1969 was trading under the name of Sandwell Garages Ltd. (*T.J.H. Price*)

A view of the Britannia Inn, 54 Parliament Street, at its junction with Trinity Road, while under the management of William Hector Spooner, 5 May 1967. Long-serving landlord Edwin Povey kept this pub during the 1920s, '30s and '40s. The last 'gaffer' to hold the licence before it closed on 29 July 1973 was George Albert Oliver. (*Andrew Maxam*)

Queen Elizabeth II coronation fancy dress party participants line up in Maud Road, near Morris Street, 2 June 1953. Back row, left to right: John Pearson, -?-, Christine Millward, June Walker, Joan Ploughman, Janet Kimes, Geoff Ploughman, Margaret Betts, June Brasnell. Front row: Denise Benbow, Carol Millward, Philip Betts, Sandra Male, Gregory Allan, Roger Harvey, Robert Kimes, Ron Summers, Chris Benbow, Hazel Birch. (*Sheila Wootton*)

The corner of Union Street was the location of this beerhouse, the Greyhound Inn, whose address was 328 Spon Lane. Horace Holder is the licensee's name above the door in this picture dating from about 1954. These premises were closed for trading on 29 January 1956, much earlier than most of the other pubs in the area. (*Andrew Maxam*)

Local children pictured at a King George VI coronation party in Morris Street on 12 May 1937. Standing on the lorry fourth from left is Jean Cleaver, and second from right is Sheila Millward. The man in the bowler hat, top right, is Jack Hammond, and in front of him are Doris Millward and Frank Guest. The girl dressed as a jockey in front of the lorry is Rita Salisbury. (*Sheila Wootton*)

The Golden Cross, 25 St Michael Street, *c*. 1980, with Bernard Patrick Bux as the landlord. Two licensees and three years later on 10 August 1983 this Ansells pub name was changed to Busby's. (*T.J.H. Price*)

The presentation of Long Service Certificates to employees of EMB Ltd, Moor Street, 1946. Back row, left to right: Alf Collins, Harold Wilkes, E. Millward, S. Key, H. Grove, George Payne, Jack Whitehouse, W. More, A. Pettitt. Third row: Fred Davies, Fred Allen, Ted Roden, Norman Noake, J. Taylor, Bert Penn, J. Bailey, Ernie Price, Charlie Scott. Second row: Fred Thompson, S. Perkins, E. Barton, H. Round, Joe Agger, Stan Simpson, Cyril Williams, G. Billington, Jack Bates, Jack Byfield. Front row: C. Williams, Arthur Bowcott, M.Sheldon, Frank Evans, R. Farmer, A. Williams, Bill Davies, H. Church, Richard Cottrell. (*David Lord*)

William and Martha Merther's off-licence, 59 Moor Street, *c.* 1960. Thomas Smith ran a general store from these premises on the corner of Bowater Street from 1914 until about 1940, before the off-licence was granted during John and Florence Bailey's sixteen year occupancy. This and the adjacent properties were demolished in 1962, thereby allowing Bowater House high-rise flats to be built on the site. (*Andrew Maxam*)

St Michael Street, 10 March 1963. After the abandonment of the two single-deck tram routes to Oldbury and Smethwick on 18 November 1929, West Bromwich Corporation replaced them with a combined bus service, later numbered 16. On the left, opposite Paradise Street, two posters are advertising the films *Gypsy* and *The Manchurian Candidate* for the Tower and Kings cinemas respectively. (*David Wilson*)

Bromford Lane looking towards Oldbury, *c.* 1926. The Turks Head, rebuilt in about 1924, is shown on the left, while, opposite, Ellen Blackwell stands on the doorstep of her post office in Barton Street. (*T.J.H. Price*)

Machine shop workers at Samuel Withers & Co., Iron Safe Manufacturers, Barton Street, *c.* 1929. Back row, left to right: Alf Sargent, Dan Munslow, John McGrotty, Frank Hall, Les Ferguson, Cyril Withers, John Hall. Fourth row: Ted Lole, ? Beresford, Louie Doleman, Arthur Roden, George Woodfield, ? Bisiker, Sam Woodfield, ? Cope, Tom Kendrick. Third row: Olive Gripton, Bill Gripton, Jack James, Billy Reeves, -?-, Bill Poulton, Ray Mantle, Bill Taylor, Richard Poulton. Second row: Jack Pickering, Tom Poxon, Jim Simkins, Jack Cook, Jack Mantle. Front row: Rose Ferguson, Ernie Hall. (*Louie Woodfield*)

Sundak FC, members of the West Bromwich Saturday League, pictured at The Hawthorns, *c.* 1958, prior to defeating Shamrock Rovers in the final of the West Bromwich Albion Shield. Back row, left to right: Les Read, Bernard Roberts, Don ?, ? Beetlestone, Abe Beetlestone, Frank Dudfield. Front row: Frank ?, Dennis Handley, Cyril Horsley, Len Winsper, Billy Hughes, Trevor Wilkes. (*Frank Dudfield*)

Paint shop employees of Samuel Withers & Co. (established 1843) Barton Street, *c.* 1929. Back row, left to right: -?-, Olive Gripton, Louie Doleman, Rose Ferguson, -?-. Third row: Beattie Hudd, -?-, Violet Kendrick, -?-, Ted Lole. Second row: -?-, Dora Wright, -?-, Irene Kendrick, -?-, Edna Kendrick, ? Lole. Front row: Alfred Beasley, ? Smith, Sandy ?. (*Louie Woodfield*)

The Dog & Duck, 58 Braybrook Street, photographed in March 1961, when Kevin Jameson was the licensee. One of Darby's beerhouses, this pub fell victim to the massive clearance and redevelopment of the Lyng area in the 1960s. These premises closed in February 1962, with Braybrook Street, Cross Street, Dove Street and Smith Street disappearing shortly afterwards. (*Sidney Darby*)

Leslie Cyril Webb, family butcher, 99a Moor Street, *c.* 1950. The business, which was acquired from Richard Thomas Mullett in 1938, carried on here for exactly twenty years before being taken over by Brian Chatwin in 1958. Four years later in 1962, when demolition of these old properties threatened, Brian moved into new premises opposite. Left to right: Brian Chatwin, Roy Sutcliffe, Leslie Webb. (*Brian Chatwin*)

The Bridge Inn, 305 Bromford Lane, when Samuel Gaynham was the landlord, 14 June 1960. Two members of the Freeman family were licensees here during a thirty-two-year period, Alfred James 1906–30 and Sarah Elizabeth 1930–8. William Stephen Joyner was the landlord when the inn closed on 6 July 1975. (*Andrew Maxam*)

Bethel Crusaders and Sunbeams pictured outside Gadds Lane Temple, 1933. Back row, left to right: Sid Nicholls, ? Mills, Jack Wood, Fred Whitehouse, ? Lloyd, Sid Hyde, Cliff Nicholls, Jack Summerhill, Fred Painter, ? Davies, George Bastable. Front row: Joe Ainge, Harry Ainge, ? Smith, Leslie Poulton, -?-, Lala Griffiths, John Spittle, -?-, ? Rees, Maurice Nicholls, Len Spittle. Pastor Rees Griffiths is in the centre of the group with Sam Linford and Claudia Griffiths either side. (*Sid Haynes*)

Devastation during the Second World War in Oak Road, at its junction with Richard Street South, on the morning of 20 November 1940. This scene followed an enemy bombing raid the previous evening at 7.10 p.m. ARP Warden Jack Aston was first at the scene, seconds after the explosion which claimed twenty-eight lives. The full ARP team stationed at B4 post in Bromford Lane was: Jack Aston, Les Bailey, Hubert Blackwell, George Handley, Arthur Pearson, George Reeves. (*South Staffs Water*)

Lodge Road looking toward the Town Hall, *c.* 1910, with Oxford Road (left) just beyond the horse-drawn bread delivery van. Izons Road is on the right. The lady dressed in white is about to enter Lodge Estate Junior & Infants School, which opened in 1904. (*T.J.H. Price*)

William Bell, in the white apron, stands on the doorstep of the Albion Hotel, 30 Paradise Street, *c.* 1908. The beer came from Thomas Oliver's brewery in Walsall Street, who no doubt supplied another of William Bell's public houses, the Grapes, 174 High Street. The Albion ceased trading on 8 March 1972, Frank Randall being the last licensee. (*Ken Rock*)

Methodists from Wesley Church, High Street march from the Oak House in May 1988 during celebrations marking the 250th anniversary of John Wesley's conversion. Pictured here in Oak Road are members of the 1st West Bromwich Brownies with Girl Guide leaders Joan Cashmore, Janet Linney and Delma Linney at the front. Walking alongside, escorting the group, is Tawny Owl Kathleen Homeshaw. (*T.J.H. Price*)

West Bromwich station, looking towards Spon Lane Bridge, *c.* 1910. Opened in 1854 it was not the first in the parish: Newton Road (1837), Bescot Junction (within the borders of West Bromwich) (1847) and Albion (1853) all preceded it. The passenger buildings shown here were demolished in 1971 with the route between Birmingham and Wolverhampton now being used by the Midland Metro tramway system. (*T.J.H. Price*)

King George VI and Queen Elizabeth are seen here in Station Mews outside West Bromwich station on 19 April 1940, before a morale-boosting tour of the town's industries. Bowing extravagantly is the Mayor of West Bromwich Cllr Edward Woodward with a uniformed Lord Dudley and George F. Darlow, the town clerk, looking on. (*T.J.H. Price*)

Fire engines were moved into the yard to make room for this party attended by firemen's children at West Bromwich fire station, Paradise Street, on Saturday 2 January 1954. Afterwards they were entertained by a film show and an illusionist, followed by a visit from Father Christmas. Marilyn Taylor is seated sixth from the right with parents Dora and Richard behind her. (*Marilyn Taylor*)

Benjamin Crowther's Station Garage and undertaking premises, 76 Paradise Street, *c.* 1920. Between 1882 and 1930 the town's fire brigade were based here in Crowther's yard, the old fire warning bell housing being visible above the roof on the top right. The new fire station, which opened nearby in 1930, was demolished in 1974. (*T.J.H. Price*)

It is unlikely that passers-by ever noticed the mock-Tudor effect on the upper frontage of Ye Olde Farriers Arms at 22 Queen Street. When this picture was taken on 26 May 1965 Margaret Murray Harris had been the licensee for over seventeen years. Raymond Harvey was the last landlord at its closure on 10 August 1969. (*Andrew Maxam*)

Christmas decorations bring a degree of cheer to these patients in the Salter Ward of Edward Street District Hospital, 1953. Margaret Scott is the first nurse on the left while Sister Green is between the other two. The 'District' was built in plain red brick between 1869 and 1871 to the design of Martin & Chamberlain of Birmingham. (*Doris Abbotts*)

Queen Street, with Walsall Street in the distance, decorated with bunting to celebrate the coronation of Queen Elizabeth II in June 1953. The Primitive Methodist Chapel on the left, originally planned as a public hall, was completed in 1847, with the major contributors being the Spittle family who were coal masters at Carters Green. The chapel was demolished in 1966. (*John Hutchcocks*)

West Bromwich Public Works FC, members of the West Bromwich Saturday League, *c.* 1957. Back row, left to right: Reg Thompson, Ken Turton, Jeff Watkins, Michael Barton, Geoff Whitehouse, Dennis Proctor, Bill Bell, Jeff Finch, George Sewell. Middle row: Terry Newell, Bill Cannon, Joe Howarth, -?-, Billy Hughes. Front row: Reg Hannington, Brian Figeon. (*Billy Hughes*)

Bull Street from Dartmouth Square, *c.* 1910. This postcard view was produced for Albert Cashmore, newsagent and stationer, whose shop at No. 4 is the first on the left. Next door, at No. 6, clothier Alf Young is making sure no one runs off with the coats he has hanging from his sign. Among the shops opposite is watchmakers Henry Haslehurst at No. 9. (*T.J.H. Price*)

A view of Bull Street from the Walsall Street end, *c.* 1965. All of the buildings shown here were demolished around 1969 prior to road widening and the construction of a multi-storey car park on the Ringway. Those out of picture on the left remain, however, but lack the character engendered by the old local shopkeepers. (*T.J.H. Price*)

The Hope & Anchor, on the corner of Bull Street and Pitt Street, March 1961, whose landlord Albert William Finney, held the licence here for fifteen years from 7 January 1954. However, when Edward Arthur Pearson succeeded him on 9 January 1969 it would only be for seven months. The pub closed on 3 August 1969 and was demolished for road widening shortly afterwards. (*Sidney Darby*)

Probably the best-known and certainly the most popular retail business in West Bromwich was Edward Trow's confectionery and ice-cream parlour. The shop at 26 Bull Street, pictured here in about 1920, was a magnet for everyone at weekends and summer bank holidays, with crowds of people queueing to buy their home-made ice-cream. (*T.J.H. Price*)

Daniel Bagnall stands outside his hardware premises at 11 Walsall Street, August 1987. He inherited the business in 1934 following the death of his father, Joseph Edward, but at that time it was located a few doors away at No. 5. The shop pictured above, which Daniel moved into during the 1940s, was a veritable time capsule of ironmongery and other household goods. After Daniel's death the building was demolished and a replica constructed at Sandwell Valley Farm. (*Edwin Yates*)

Joseph Edward Bagnall, seen here on the right, commissioned this photograph of his premises at No. 5 Walsall Street in 1930. The business was originally established at 233 Spon Lane around 1894, with Joseph moving to the shop pictured left shortly afterwards. (*T.J.H. Price*)

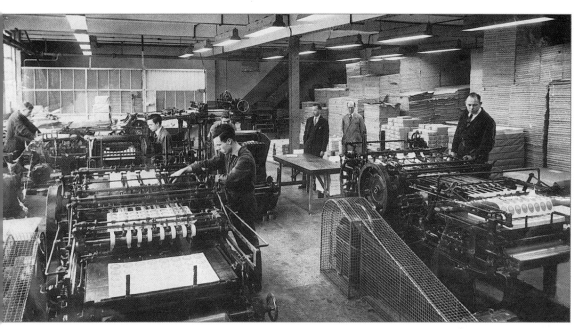

The machine room of Joseph Wones Ltd., printers, of 41 Walsall Street, *c.* 1948. Second from the right is shop foreman John Baggott who worked at the company for a magnificent fifty-four years. He was awarded the Military Medal and Bar while serving in the Grenadier Guards as a stretcher-bearer during the First World War. (*Joan Oldhams*)

Wones United FC, undefeated 1969/70 champions of Premier Division One in the West Bromwich Sunday League. Back row, left to right: David Garrett, Don Priest, Fred Hughes, Philip 'Chick' Bates, John South, John Morris, Peter Bartram, Cliff Priest, Geoff Spicer. Front row: Barry Stokes, Pat Molloy, Derek White, Brian Markham (captain), Bobby Shinton, Gordon Lee, Brian Hampson. (*Brian Markham*)

High Street at the junction with Scotland Passage on the right, *c.* 1935. The row of shops pictured includes Montague Burton who is advertising made-to-measure suits for 37s; Foster Brothers, clothiers; Marks & Spencer's Bazaar; Dunn & Co., hatters; and George Mason, grocer. Many will remember Melba's the milliner opposite at No. 158 and Mabel Voce the proprietress. (*T.J.H. Price*)

This picture from about 1920 shows, on the immediate right of the High Street at No. 91, the premises of stationer Henry Herbert Prince who in 1924, while representing the Lyng Ward on the Local Council, wrote a history of the town entitled *Old West Bromwich*. (*T.J.H. Price*)

The High Street with Hudson's Passage on the right, *c.* 1955. The passage was named after Robert Spear Hudson, the inventor of Hudson's Dry Soap Powder, who in 1845 was trading as a chemist in the High Street. In about 1875 he opened a factory in Liverpool and, together with his works in Hudson's Passage, began exporting his product all over the world. *(T.J.H. Price)*

The annual party for children and employees of F.W. Woolworth & Co., 180–2 High Street, held at Grant Hall, Christmas 1953. Among those in the photograph are: Jean May, Walter Harper, Joan Harper, Sheila May, Joyce Hill, Evelyn Stapenhill, Brenda Powis, Betty Blewitt, Joyce Hill, Olive Hill, Daisy Hill, Olive Shivlock, Brenda Millward, Agness Green, Olive Saunders, Irene Latimer, Dorothy Jordan, Betty Wright, Brenda Stapenhill, Violet Parkes. *(Walter Harper)*

Employees of F.W. Woolworth & Co pose for a photograph outside their premises at 180–2 High Street before departing on an outing to Blackpool in 1953. Among those in the back row: Daisy Hill, Margaret Knowles, Olive Hill. Middle row: Jean Millward, Joyce Hill, Sid Facer, Betty Cox. Front row: Hazel Finch, Dorothy Gilbert, Alice Woodbridge, Miss Beeson, Gwen Powis, Mr Underhill. (*Margaret Culwick*)

The new Market Hall situated between High Street and Paradise Street near Woolworths. In this picture, taken shortly before the hall closed in 1973, Fred Evans is seen pushing a trolley just below the sign bearing his name. This wooden structure was built in 1922 as a replacement for the old Market Hall, which had closed sixteen years earlier. (*T.J.H. Price*)

Pupils of the Arcadian School of Dancing, situated above the Arcade, Paradise Street, pictured at an award winners presentation evening, *c.* 1963. The owners, Laurie Hughes and Stella Brookes were also joined by the mayor of West Bromwich, Cllr John Evans, third from the right. Margaret Morgan is third from the left, back row, while Laurie Hughes is below the sign on the right. (*Margaret Morgan*)

The 10th West Bromwich Boys and the 4th Walsall Girls Brigades marching down the High Street in the West Bromwich Carnival of about 1973. Among those in the band are: Susanne Withers, Diane Tay, Susan Tay, Leslie Dyke, Malcolm Dyke, John Bunyard, Richard Mayhew, Tony Gibbard, Janet Fellows, Jim Gibbons. Ada Dyke is following behind. (*Ada Dyke*)

High Street, *c.* 1964. The tall K & J building in the centre background was demolished in 2002 to make way for the new Astle Park Retail and Leisure Complex, presently under construction. The only High Street retailer in this picture still trading is Bell & Jones,who now occupy premises at 33 Queens Square. (*Edwin Yates*)

A magnificent view of William Joseph Pester's greengrocery shop on the corner of High Street and Queen Street, *c.* 1930. The business moved here in the 1880s from 4 Bull Street, where around 1872 a William Pester was trading as a bird fancier and dealer. (*T.J.H. Price*)

Henry Edward Bradsworth's fruiterer's shop, 244 High Street, *c.* 1910. The business dates back to the 1860s when Henry's father also had premises in Walsall Street. Bradsworth's was succeeded at this location by Thompson & Rose, also fruiterers, and finally a McDonald's restaurant. Note the cash register in the outside display. (*T.J.H. Price*)

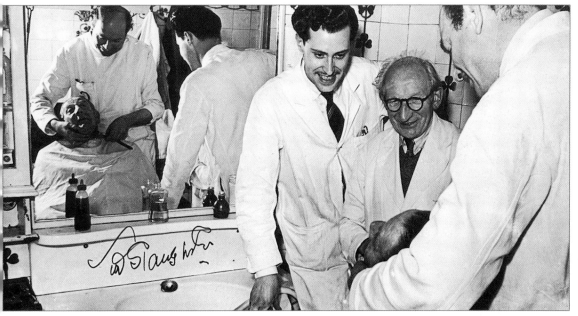

Cammies & Cadman, ladies and gentlemen's hairdressing salon, 220 High Street, *c.* 1951. This business was established at 40 Paradise Street, *c.* 1930, by John Harry Cammies who later took over the above High Street premises in 1950. The man being shaved with an open razor is actor Todd Slaughter *The Demon Barber of Fleet Street*, who was appearing locally at the Plaza Theatre. Left to right: Ted Drew, Harold Bramley, John Harry Cammies. (*Michael Cammies*)

Bell & Jones, chemists and photographic dealers, 275 High Street, *c.* 1965. This firm was established in 1932 after taking over from Galloways Stores, who themselves had succeeded drapers Dain & Morgan at this address. On 31 May 1968 the business was purchased by Messrs D. & S. Peakman who three years later, on 10 June 1971, relocated to Queens Square. (*Terry Brown*)

Samuel Greenway (right) looks out from his ironmongery shop at 231 High Street, *c.* 1905. What a wonderful display of household goods and tools there are here with shovels ranging from 1*s* to 2*s* 9*d*! Business could not have been all that good however, because this limited company had disappeared from the records by 1908. (*T.J.H. Price*)

Replacing tramlines in the High Street at the junction of New Street and St Michael Street in preparation for the electrification of the tramway system, which was opened to the public on 20 December 1903. Note the Star & Garter pub on the left and St Michael's Roman Catholic Church before the addition of the tower and spire. (*T.J.H. Price*)

The High Street pictured in about 1923, twenty years after the top photograph was taken from a similar position. St Michael's Roman Catholic Church tower and spire, designed by architect Edmund Kirby and added in 1911, is of Ruabon brick and Hollington stone. After major alterations the church was subsequently consecrated in 1917. (*T.J.H. Price*)

The confectionery and tobacconist's shop of Thomas Howard Homeshaw, 19 New Street, *c.* 1930. A fine example of the temptations confronting youngsters in the thirties and with the inevitable special offer of bottle sweets at 5½d per pound. Thomas bought the business as a going concern in 1927 but it was his wife Florrie, pictured in the doorway, who effectively ran the shop. When they left in 1951 it was sold to shoe retailer Jack Wassell. (*Kathleen Homeshaw*)

An out-of-service Birmingham Corporation tramcar glides along the High Street towards Dartmouth Square to begin the short-working No. 77 service to Birmingham, *c.* 1938. Partly obscured by the tram are the premises of watchmaker Hubert Charles at No. 271. (*National Tramway Museum*)

The Acorn Inn, 107 New Street, pictured here on 9 November 1968, was previously a Darby's house with a reputation for long-serving landlords. Edward Perry for example held the licence for over twenty years from 1922, while Alan Peniket served for another eleven up to the pub's closure on 30 April 1969. (*Andrew Maxam*)

Nurses and members of the St John Ambulance Brigade are seen here marching down New Street during 'Wings for Victory' week, 5–12 June 1943. The objective, through national savings, was to raise money for the purchase of Spitfire aircraft during the Second World War. The Nelson Pub is next to the post office in the background. (*Ray Gough*)

Another New Street pub, the Roebuck Inn at No. 133, is pictured here on the corner of Walsall Street on 27 April 1962. At this time the licensee was Benjamin Hamblett. All of these properties were swept away during the late 1960s and early 1970s, and a car park now occupies the site. (*Bill Inkson*)

Cllr Arthur Medley, the Mayor of West Bromwich, presents certificates to prize-winners during the YMCA carnival held in Dartmouth Park on 15 June 1951. At the microphone is George Salter School woodwork teacher Edgar Bloor with Jesse Medley, the Mayoress, on the right. (*Jim Medley*)

The New Street entrance to Dartmouth Park, *c.* 1922, with Seagar and Gregory Streets off to the left and right respectively. In 1877 Lord Dartmouth gave 56 acres of land from his estate for use as a public park, which opened here in 1878. It was further enlarged in 1887 by the gift of another 9½ acres. (*Fred Dyson*)

Dartmouth Park paddling pool, *c.* 1930. The park was opened by Lord Dartmouth on 3 June 1878 on a 99-year lease. However, on 2 July 1919 both he and Viscount Lewisham generously gave the freehold to the borough. The deed of conveyance was presented to the mayor, Cllr John Bell JP, by HRH the Prince of Wales on 13 June 1923. (*T.J.H. Price*)

High Street, Wesley's production of the pantomime *Cinderella, c.* 1953. Back row, left to right: Jean Saunders, Brenda Batten, Ken Dunn, Dorothy Smith, -?-, Eric Fieldhouse, Alan Udall, Eileen Roe, Eve Cook, Nellie Saunders. Third row: -?-, -?-, Anne Ryder, Gillian Hancox, -?-, Stan Hope, Jean Smith, Gladys Slater, Dennis Vaughan. Second row: Murielle Smith, Rhona Cook, Valerie Dyke, Gillian Wharton, Janet Neale, Vivien Ault, Christine Ryder. Front row: Carol Whitehouse, -?-, Leslie Duncombe, -?-, -?-, -?-, Linda Neale, Susan Whitehouse. (*Dorothy Smith*)

Wesley Church, High Street, Sunday School Anniversary, *c.* 1948. Back row, left to right: John Cooper, Charles Booth, Arthur Newey, Haddon Onions, Avril Horne, Rene Saunders. Among the fourth row are: Terry Brown, Beryl Thompson, Millie Newey, Margaret Wall, Eileen Roe. (*Beryl Price*)

The 5th West Bromwich Boys Brigade football team based at Wesley Church, *c.* 1987. Back row, left to right: David Butler, David Bevan, Andrew Barnfield, Darren Cooper, Neil White, Jason Staphnill, Paul Exhall, Michael Barrett. Front row: Dean Exhall, Lee Bennett, Karl Cooper, Martyn Reynolds, Jason May. (*T.J.H. Price*)

Wesley Church, High Street, Sunday School Anniversary, *c.* 1955. Back row, left to right: -?-, Arthur Newey, Cecil Hancox, Tom Saunders, Geoff Ault, -?-, Maurice Pikett, Jack Mason, Jim Overton. Eighth row: -?-, Rose Harris, Dorothy Wilkins, Freda Hockley, Emmie Adams, Gwen Cook, Nellie Saunders, Kathleen Fieldhouse, Phyllis Ault, Daisy Rowley, ? Holden, Rene Saunders, -?-. Seventh row: Kathleen Homeshaw, Brenda Batten, Evelyn Cook, Jean Smith, Margaret Chambers, Tessa Douglas, Heather Rowley, Beryl Simmons, Dorothy Smith, Murielle Smith. Among the fifth row: Beryl Thompson, Margaret Ryder, Carol Hughes. Centre: Revd Handel Broadbent. (*Beryl Price*)

High Street looking towards Victoria Street, *c.* 1954. Kenrick & Jefferson Ltd., founded in 1878, opened the first of their two buildings on the left of the picture in 1883 with the second following in 1928. Opposite, the premises of the Midland Electricity Board were later demolished and replaced with an Allied Carpets showroom. (*T.J.H. Price*)

Willans Brothers, mineral water manufacturers of Bromford Lane, provided the transport for the West Bromwich Food Office's entry in the town's carnival in about 1948. Their float, pictured here in the High Street passing the Army & Navy Stores and the Arcade (top left), won first prize for this effort. (*T.J.H. Price*)

The elaborate frontage of house furnishers Hill & Long at 310–14 High Street catches the eye in this photograph dating from around 1964. The firm was established in 1887 by John Hill, a bedding manufacturer of 120 High Street, with Mr Long joining later. It ceased trading in the 1970s and afterward became the Lombard Shopping Mall within the Bassi Group. (*Edwin Yates*)

Cllr Arthur Medley, Mayor of West Bromwich, reads the Proclamation of Queen Elizabeth II's accession to the throne from a specially erected platform in front of the Town Hall on 8 February 1952. Among those behind: Jesse Medley the Mayoress, George Jones, Harry Sower, Minnie Evitts, Ernie Lissimore and George Salter school teacher Reg Turley in a scouts uniform. (*T.J.H. Price*)

The upper floor of this 1955 view of Ruskin Hall, the imposing building immediately left, was once known as Gripton's Commercial College, the principal being James Gripton. His other business interests are reflected in his ownership of the three properties below, Griptons Radio & Television Stores, Griptons Confectionery and the property leased by him to M. & E. Woodhall, fancy drapers. (*T.J.H. Price*)

West Bromwich gas showroom was severely damaged after an enemy bombing raid on the town during the evening of 19 November 1940. This picture, taken the following morning outside what was left of their High Street premises, shows some of the devastation. (*South Staffs Water*)

Lombard Street looking towards Bratt Street on the morning of 20 November 1940. Along with the High Street and Oak Road this part of the town also suffered from the previous night's air raid and it was thought at the time that German bombers were attempting to destroy the nearby railway line. (*South Staffs Water*)

Head Postmaster, Major Ken Heal, presents the Imperial Service Medal to Horace Victor Doughty at West Bromwich Postal Sorting Office in 1966 for completing forty-six years of service. Left to right: Major Ken Heal, Arthur Wakelam, Horace Doughty, Joe Brookes, Ken Brown, Harry Mann, Albert Gumberell, Harry Medley, Ron White. (*Alf Perks*)

Lower High Street at Sandwell Road, *c.* 1910. William Almond, bookseller and stationer, occupies the corner premises at No. 245, above which many years later was painted the word 'Rechabites'. This referred to the Independent Order of Rechabites, which was established in England in about 1681, but became a teetotal benefit society after 1835. (*T.J.H. Price*)

The New Hippodrome music hall, Lower High Street, *c.* 1907. This replacement for an earlier theatre was opened in 1906 by a company called 'Sites Limited', with Albert Withers installed here as the manager. It also began showing films in about 1918 but closed in 1922, demolition taking place shortly afterwards. Guest Motors eventually acquired the site, which became their sales area for used cars. (*T.J.H. Price*)

Mary Firkin's 'celebrated' pork pie shop, 25 Carters Green, *c.* 1908. Dating from about 1850, when it was owned by two unmarried sisters named Welch, the business was eventually sold to a Florence Firkin by James Welch in 1894. Firkin's were renowned for winning a gold medal for their pork pies at the Royal Agricultural Hall, London in September 1907. (*T.J.H. Price*)

Shaftesbury Street from the High Street, *c.* 1948. George Mason's shop on the left (No. 377) was purchased by Guest Motors in 1950 as part of their refurbishment programme which extended their showroom and office accommodation. (*Peter Guest*)

Harry Wallett's newsagents, stationery and fancy goods shop, 43 Carters Green, pictured during 'Civic Week', 26 February to 5 March 1927. These premises had been in the hands of the Wallett family for over forty years, when they were sold around 1961. Their daughter Dorothy was an infants' teacher at Fisher Street School, Great Bridge, during the 1940s.
(*Iris Reynolds*)

Frank Guest's original showroom frontage facing Lower High Street, *c.* 1925. The above premises were purchased in 1922, seven years after obtaining the Ford franchise. Although they withdrew from selling cars in August 1999 their commercial vehicle business is still operating in Kenrick Way. (*Peter Guest*)

The Nags Head, 15 Dudley Street, next to Carters Green Passage, March 1961, when Harry William Hadley was the licensee. There would be only two more landlords to hold the licence at this Darby's house before closure on 2 November 1969. They were Brian Devaney, 26 September 1963 and Raymond Dunn, 25 July 1968. (*Sidney Darby*)

The Black Cock, 76 Guns Lane, 3 August 1968, when John Leslie Peace was the licensee. After Enterprise Inns had purchased these premises from Bass on 26 March 1992, no less than fourteen licensees were to pass through its doors before it was sold for conversion to residential use on 20 September 2002. Gurmeyo Kaur Mahal was the last. (*Alan Price*)

Madeleine Carroll, actress, was born on 26 February 1906 at 32 Herbert Street, West Bromwich, to parents Helene and John Carroll, her father being a schoolmaster at the West Bromwich Municipal Secondary School. The birth certificate shows, however, that her first names were in fact Edith Madeleine, and her French-born mother's maiden name was recorded as Tuaillon. Shortly afterwards the family moved to No. 7 Jesson Street, where Madeleine spent most of her childhood – a far cry from the glamorous world of Hollywood that she was later to encounter. After gaining her BA from Birmingham University in 1926 she became a teacher for a short while, but it was her desire to act that occupied her thoughts above everything else. She was eventually offered a part in a touring production of *Mr What's His Name*, which subsequently led to her West End début in *The Lash*. Her first film role was in *The Guns at Loos*, shown at the Imperial Cinema, West Bromwich, in February 1929. The film she will always be remembered for however (which is still shown on television from time to time) is Alfred Hitchcock's *The Thirty-Nine Steps*, in which she co-starred with Robert Donat. This was the film shown on the opening night of the Tower Cinema on Monday 9 December 1935. Madeleine Carroll's last film was Otto Preminger's *The Fan* made in 1949. After four marriages – to Philip Astley, Henry Lavorel, Sterling Hayden and publisher Andrew Heiskell – Madeleine eventually moved to Marbella, Spain, where she died in October 1987. (*T.J.H. Price*)

An extract from the Tower Cinema's opening night souvenir programme. (*T.J.H. Price*)

The Clock Tower at Carters Green, *c.* 1932. This magnificent timepiece was erected in 1897 to honour Great Bridge-born Reuben Farley, the town's greatest benefactor and five times Mayor of West Bromwich. On the left is Arthur Rowley's Billiard Hall, which was demolished in 1935 allowing the Tower Cinema to be built on the site. (*Ken Rock*)

Carters Green at the junction of Dudley Street (left) and Old Meeting Street (right), *c.* 1930. The Methodist Chapel, in the background was built on the site of the old Junction Inn, a recognised calling house for vehicular traffic between Birmingham and the North. The chapel opened on Monday 8 May 1876, closed in about 1949 and was demolished in 1970. (*T.J.H. Price*)

Carters Green from Old Meeting Street, *c.* 1964, showing one of the area's best known retail outlets, Pawsons Family Stores and pawnbrokers, which dates from about 1926. The Clock Tower Restaurant, third left, was formerly the British Restaurant, and before that a drill hall. *How The West Was Won* starring John Wayne was being shown at the Tower Cinema on the right. (*Edwin Yates*)

This unusual night-time picture shows Tyndal Street decorated for the coronation of King George VI and Queen Elizabeth in May 1937. On the doorstep of the Plumbers Arms pub at No. 36 is the licensee Jack Pedley with industrialist Jack Fitzpatrick next to him. (*Gordon Parker*)

The Talbot Hotel (The Lamp), 62 Dudley Street, *c.* 1980, one of the few licensed premises in West Bromwich to have been listed as a hotel since at least 1870. Edward Raymond Hughes was landlord when this picture was taken with John Summerfield being the last when it closed in 1994. (*T.J.H. Price*)

Bert Parker in the short trousers is seen here receiving the borough's first prize certificate from Cllr Ruth Parfitt for the decorations in Tyndal Street marking the coronation of Queen Elizabeth II on 2 June 1953. Also in the picture, fourth, fifth and sixth from the left on the front row are, Jesse Medley, Philip Taylor and Reg Thompson (face obscured) who designed the display. (*Gordon Parker*)

West Bromwich Transport's Coronation Bus outside George Hill's Motor Coach Tours premises in Old Meeting Street during May 1953. This vehicle, which was illuminated at night, also travelled the borough each December wishing its townspeople a 'Happy Christmas'. Sadly, this pre-war tradition died out during the 1960s. (*Margaret Tupper*)

What a wonderful example of a George Hill's charabanc, pictured here parked outside Harry Wallet's newsagents shop on Carters Green, *c.* 1930! George Hill's daughter Ann (Aston) was a hostess on Bob Monkhouse's television programme *The Golden Shot* during the 1960s. (*Iris Reynolds*)

Chapter Two
Great Bridge, Greets Green & Swan Village

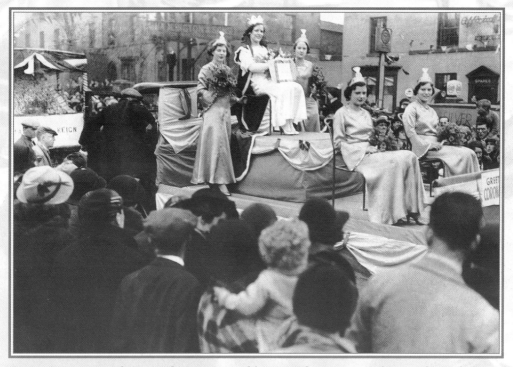

Greets Green Carnival Queen Clara Bryan and her attendants are seen here in the High Street, taking part in the town's celebrations marking the coronation of King George VI and Queen Elizabeth on 12 May 1937. Back row, left to right: Irene Magee, Clara Bryan, Edna Slim. Front row: Molly Onions, Ida Mackay. (*T.J.H. Price*)

The main road through Great Bridge, at its junction with Whitehall Road, March 1981. On the immediate left, Tesco Stores had just vacated their property, which was previously occupied by Victor Value Supermarket. Most of the shops in this block were built in 1963 on the site of the Palace Cinema, which closed on 16 April 1960. (*Frank Wardle*)

Licensee Kathleen Hoskins was in residence when this picture was taken of the Wagon & Horses Commercial Hotel in 1965. This old coaching inn was built in 1764 to take advantage of the London to Shrewsbury coach traffic using the realigned main road through Great Bridge and many people were disappointed that such an historic building was not saved from demolition back in the 1970s. (*Jim Houghton*)

An ex-Wolverhampton bus in the new livery of West Midlands Passenger Transport Executive has just turned into Whitehall Road on the Great Bridge to Yew Tree Estate, No. 2 route, 31 May 1975. The row of buildings on the left, containing Rose and William Homer's florist shop, are very different today having undergone a considerable structural make-over. (*David Wilson*)

Greets Green Domino League Cup winning team, Royal Oak, assembles in the bar for a photograph, *c.* 1957. Ann and Ted Penny were licensees of this Whitehall Road pub at the time. Back row, left to right: Sid Willetts, Horace Davies, Billy Walker, -?-. Second row: John Wherton, Ernie Parkes, -?-, Sam Price. Front row: Wilf Evans, Arthur Howes, and Fred Rollinson. (*T.J.H. Price*)

William Street looking towards Charles Street, 20 July 1968. The Ansells Plough & Harrow pub on the right was not long away from demolition when this photograph was taken, George Eaton being the last licensee. This was once a populous street with a vibrant community spirit, but now only industrial properties are to be found here. (*Alan Price*)

Braithwaite FC, from Henry Street, members of the West Bromwich Saturday League, *c.* 1959. Back row, left to right: Les Hill, Billy Hodgkins, Roland Prentice, Alan Shermer, Fred Bradley, Alan Bird. Front row: Brian Fellows John Edwards, Kenneth Lawley, Peter Wilkes, George 'Sparrow' Wright, Jack Shermer. (*John Edwards*)

The (top) Beehive, 112 Brickhouse Lane, July 1976 when Alan Causer was the licensee. Curiously, this was one of two 'Beehive' pubs built only a few hundred yards from each other. On the left is the entrance to the 'Cracker', which was a favourite haunt of courting couples. (*T.J.H. Price*)

An outing from the (top) Beehive, Brickhouse Lane, to Southend 18 June 1950. Back row, left to right: -?-, Joe Wright Snr, Anna Dixon, Mary Wright, Gertie Cartwright, Flossie Baker, -?-, Elizabeth McGuire (licensee), -?-, Annie Wright, -?-, Joe Howell, Lucy Evans, -?-, Ann Whittingham, -?-, -?-, Iris Hendon, -?-. Front row: Joe Wright Jnr, George Dixon, Tom Cartwright, Jim Baker, Jack Brown, Arthur Evans, George Fullwood, -?-, Leslie Howell, Ted Hill. (*Irene Stott*)

An ex-West Bromwich Corporation Daimler CVG6/30 bus in the cream and dark blue colours of the West Midlands Passenger Transport Executive turns into Brickhouse Lane, Great Bridge on the No. 19 Oldbury to Stone Cross route, 18 March 1976. This service terminated at Hill Top when it was introduced in 1925, but was afterwards extended to Stone Cross in October 1932. (*David Wilson*)

Ron Harrison, managing director of Great Bridge Foundry, Sheepwash Lane, hosted this Christmas party for his employees' children at Grant Hall, West Bromwich, in 1951. Among those in the picture are Christine Adams, John Adams, Paul Cox, Pat Price, Rose Price, Valerie Price. (*Sam Price*)

A side view of the Queens Head, 93 Cophall Street, *c.* 1961. Opened on 5 January 1961 with Samuel Gaynham as the first landlord, it was built to replace 'Tommy Wrights' Queens Head pub in nearby Horton Street. Glynis Carol Bennett was the last licensee before demolition on 15 August 1997. (*Andrew Maxam*)

Residents in and around the Newtown area of Great Bridge line up for a photograph during the King George VI coronation celebrations on 12 May 1937. Among those on the left: Jean Earp, Albert Earp, David Freeman, May Stimpson, Bill Bennett, Ann Wright. Centre: Hannah Phillips, Eddie Phillips, Joyce Phillips, Lily Phillips, Alice Toon. Right: Florence Dickinson, Ann Connor, Daisy Toon, Rose Stott, Joan Phillips, Ada Dickinson, May Bennett, Irene Stott, Winnie Freeman. (*Irene Stott*)

Wellington Tube Works, Brickhouse Lane, annual dinner at the Station Hotel, Dudley, *c.* 1948. Among the fourth row are: Ken Lloyd, David Corfield, Joe Smith, Iris Beckley, Laurence Garner, Clarice Sim. Third row: Donald Blocksidge, Irene Simpkin, Tom Evans, Ted Nuttall, -?-, Edna Taylor, Ray Wagstaff, Lelia Woodhall, Ray Greenway, Audrey Small, -?-, -?-. Among the second row: Beattie Arch, Winnie Shelton, Joan Homer. Front row: John Thom, Lou Stanton, Sam Fisher, George Hadley. (*Audrey Small*)

Presentation of Long Service Awards to Wellington Tube Works employees, Brickhouse Lane, *c.* 1952. Back row, second from right: Stan Holland. Middle row: -?-, Jim Latham, -?-, -?-, Tom Allen, Billy Griffiths. Front row: George Whatnall, Tom 'Flick' Jeavons, Douglas Turner, James T.E. Masters, Peter Black, Cyril Turner. (*Joyce Ferrington*)

Employees of the Wellington Tube Works, Great Bridge, at Abergele summer camp August 1945. Back row, left to right: -?-, Stan Bratt, Bill Bolton, Ken Jeavons, Jim Barnfield, Selwyn ?, Ron Dudley, -?-, Alan Whale, -?-, -?-, -?-, -?-, Desmond Allen, Victor Sims, Frank Wagstaff, John Parry, Ray Wagstaff, Howard Clarke, ? Parry, -?-, Len Jones. Front row: -?-, Eva Dolman, Dorothy Talbot, Jean ?, Jean?, Billy Broughton, -?-, -?-, -?-, -?-, -?-, Brenda Mayo, -?-, -?-, Doris Haines, -?-, -?-, -?-, Lillian Green, Joan Whitehouse, Evelyn Moore. (*Doris Smith*)

A Birmingham Corporation No. 74 bus on the Dudley–Birmingham route picks up passengers outside the machinery showrooms of Messrs B.O. Hulbert, 19 Great Bridge, 3 March 1963. Between 1892 and 1918 these premises were known as William Poultons' Pianoforte Warehouse, one of the largest in the Midlands. All of the properties shown here have since been replaced by a car park. (*David Wilson*)

Roy Dursley is holding the Union Flag in this picture of a St Peter's Church carnival float in Whitehall Road, *c.* 1937. Also on the lorry, which was provided by A.H. Adams & Sons, of Great Bridge, is Captain Willoughby Allway's son David, second from the right in a bishop's hat. Barbara Breatt was the carnival queen on this occasion. (*David Allway*)

St Peter's Church bible class photographed in the Church Army Social Centre grounds, Whitehall Road, *c.* 1930. Captain Willoughby Allway held these classes in the 'Tin Hut' from 1926 until his retirement to Smethwick in 1954. Back row, left to right: -?-, -?-, -?-, -?-, ? Fenton, ? Ince, Norman Hirons, -?-. Middle row: -?-, ? Sheridan, Captain Willoughby Allway, Dick Turner, Herbert Saunders, -?-. (*David Allway*)

Lily Holyhead, Carnival Queen of St Peter's Church, Whitehall Road, with her attendants, *c*. 1945. Left to right: Mary Gwinett, Fred Price, Lily Holyhead, Ivy Tinson, Barbara Richards, -?-, Flossie Eccles, Joan Guy, Betty Hodnet, Lily Lloyd. (*Brenda Nicklin*)

Salem Congregational Church, Sheepwash Lane, Sunday School Anniversary, 17 June 1956. Back row, left to right: Manny Wright, Joyce Roberts, Cynthia Moore, Margaret Whitehouse, Brenda Williams, ? Goode, Iris Day, Dora Day, Albert Ball, Harry Jones. Fourth row: Gloria Sansome, -?-, Brenda Whitehouse, -?-, Vera Blakesley, Sandra Webb, Horace Parkes, -?-, -?-, -?-, -?-, Valerie Webb, Maureen Webb, Margaret Johnson. Among the third row: Pat York, Janet Fletcher, Joy Heath, Valerie Roberts, Ken Serrell, Graham Jones. Front row: Margaret Aston, Diane Bagnall, Sandra Woodhall, Rosalind Roberts. (*Colin Aston*)

Swan Village gas tank dominates this view of Phoenix Street taken on 4 September 1968. This gasholder was built in 1928 and, after surviving German bombing raids during the Second World War, was finally blown up by Transco on 5 September 1999. (*Alan Price*)

Swan Village Methodist Church, Dudley Street, Sunday School Anniversary, *c.* 1967. Back row, left to right: Rosemary Morton, Margaret Morgan, Mavis Scott, Yvonne Russell, Sylvia Withey, Lorna Scott, Denise Lennard, Sandra Hughes. Third row: -?-, Karen Lennard, Dawn Perry, -?-, -?-, Pat Martin, Robert Toovey, Clive Campbell, Irene Fenton, Angela Bullock, Carol Williams, Amanda Toovey, Millicent Seville. Among the second row: David Welch, Jean Toovey, Jennifer Howard, Gillian Harvey. Among the front row: Susan Williams, Peter Welch, Dawn Howard, Ian Glover, Diane Williams. Right: Bert Elwell (seated), Tom Dunn. (*Margaret Morgan*)

An ex-GWR 'Hall' class 4–6–0 No. 6907 *Davenham Hall* locomotive heading a passenger train passes through Swan Village main line station travelling north toward Wolverhampton on 7 May 1961. This line closed in 1972, the last day of service being on 4 March. (*David Williams*)

Swan Village Methodist Church Women's Bright Hour production of *The Village Wedding, c.* 1932. Back row, left to right: Annie Sparrow, -?-, -?-, Elizabeth Ellison, -?-, -?-, Elizabeth Knight, Ann ?, -?-, Lily Ore, George Barnes, Florrie Edmunds. Front row: Rebecca Roberts, Gertie Edmunds, -?-, Agness Scarlett, Vera Bullock, May Jones, -?-, ? Tycer, -?-. (*Maureen Morgan*)

Whitehall Road, Greets Green, at the junction of Whitgreave Street, 8 March 1964. This shopping centre, brewery and schools had completely disappeared by the end of the 1970s, leaving the local community with a sense of sadness at their loss. The Primitive Methodist Chapel, previously located where the cars are parked, was demolished some years earlier in 1958. (*David Wilson*)

Albion Globetrotters FC, Greets Green, members of the Birmingham Youth Committee League, 1952/3. Back row, left to right: F. Williams, Stan Downing, Norman Lester, Geoff Plested, Brian Wyres, John Smith, Don Wilkes. Front row: Alan Burrows, Stan Flukes, Gordon Troath (captain), Ron Aston, Colin Bromley. Brian Wyres, the goalkeeper, signed amateur forms for West Bromwich Albion during this season. (*Stan Downing*)

An ex-West Bromwich Corporation bus in the livery of WMPE, on the No. 4 Dartmouth Square–Great Bridge route via Greets Green, enters Whitehall Road on 11 June 1975. Ryders Green Methodist Church, built in1874, is on the left while opposite, on the corner of Oldbury Road, part of the Union Cross pub is just visible. (*David Wilson*)

Church Army Social junior football team, during the 1952/3 season. Back row, left to right: Archie Read, ? Jukes, Geoff Plested, Jimmy Gittins, -?-, Maurice Watson, Freddy Turton. Front row: Billy Richards, Don Read, Ray Whale, Frank Holloway, Chris Whitehouse, -?-. Ray Whale afterwards signed professional forms for West Bromwich Albion.
(*Geoff Plested*)

The Union Cross public house, 2 Oldbury Road, Greets Green, 6 August 1965. This Butlers house was previously owned by the Bowen family who also had their own brewery at the rear of these premises. At the time of this picture Frances Ann Maddox was the licensee, with Doris Annie Booker being the last when it closed on 4 April 1984. (*Andrew Maxam*)

Union Celtic FC, pictured at the Hawthorns in 1962, before their Albion Shield final against St Paul's (Golds Hill). Back row, left to right: -?-, Keith Fellows, John Fellows, John Austin, Don Parkes, Sid Walker, Joe Howes. Front row: Gerry Arnold, Billy Hughes, Arthur Parsons, Ronnie Evans, George Millward, Alan Burgess. (*Billy Hughes*)

The Eight Locks, 1 Ryders Green Road, March 1961. Jack Judge, the Oldbury singer and songwriter, used to perform here. Legend has it that on New Year's Day 1912 someone bet him that he could not write a song and perform it that same day. He won the wager by instantly composing, and afterwards singing, 'It's a Long Way to Tipperary' at the Grand Theatre in Stalybridge. (*Sidney Darby*)

Committee and club members of the Greets Green Liberal Club, Whitehall Road, make merry behind the bar during Christmas, *c.* 1965. Left to right: Edna Scragg, Sheila Burgess, Sam Whitehouse, Cilla Burgess, Joan France, Muriel Smith, Maud Copper. (*Muriel Smith*)

Legendary Tipton athlete Jack Holden performs the ceremony of crowning Rita Hill, the Greets Green Primitive Methodist Church Carnival Queen, on Saturday 3 October 1953. Left to right: Jack Holden, H. Thomas, Rita Hill, David Round, Ivy Round. (*Rita Welch*)

Youth and senior teams of Greets Green Prims FC, 1955/6 season. Back row, left to right: Reg Bannister, Harry Bird, Harold Lester, Jack Aspley, Billy Todd, Arthur Bishton. Third row: David Nightingale, Tom Dyke, Dennis Bratt, Jack Dyke, Tony Welch, Howard Holland, Alan Griffiths, John Lewis, Jimmy Cox, Tommy Meek, Brian Harley, Tony Moore, Brian Aston, Alan Fullwood, Ron Bates, Tom Hughes, David Dyke, Ernie Ainge, Joe Dyke. Second row: Billy Smith, Colin Whitehouse, Terry Talbot, Ron Bowen. Front row: Graham Dyke, Trevor Woolley, Keith Slater, John Ainge. (*David Dyke*)

The Evergreens' production of *Sinbad the Sailor* at Greets Green Primitive Methodist Church, *c.* 1949. Back row, left to right: Wilf Parkes, Olive Spink, Dorothy Cooksey, Dennis Woodall, Doreen Cox, Jean Beddow, Brenda Arnold, Howard Parker, Albert Farmer, Hazel Jackson, John Smith. Front row: Joan Smith, Sheila Capewell, Betty Clapham, Stan Dodd, Norma Charlton, Beattie Dodd, Betty Jeavons. (*Joan Howes*)

Greets Green Primitive Methodist Church Carnival Queen, Iris Howes, leads her entourage through Farley Park prior to the crowning ceremony, 1 October 1949. Among those following are Anne Round, Janet Thomas, Diane Winchurch, Beryl Woolley, Sheila Capewell, Mary Howes, Josie Green, Betty Clapham, Norma Charlton, Joyce Lester, Brenda Arnold, Jean Beddow, Dorothy Cooksey, Ivy Round, Marjorie Fieldhouse, Sheila Price. (*John Howes*)

Albion railway station looking south towards Birmingham, *c.* 1957. The station, which was on the Stour Valley line, opened in 1853 some twelve months before the town centre had this facility. Passenger services were withdrawn from here in 1960, with freight ceasing by 1964. (*Stations UK*)

Izons FC, members of the Wolverhampton & District Works Amateur Football League, 1935/6. Back row, left to right: Tom Cox, -?-, -?-, -?-. Middle row: Charles Poole, Ted Brookes, Jack Wherton, Horace Grainger, Edward Cox, Harry Garratt, -?-, -?-, -?-. Front row: Cllr Arthur Smith, Merry Wherton, William Pitt, Captain John Izon Cheshire, -?-, -?-, Harry Hill, Jack Gibbs. (*Edgar Cox*)

Chapter Three

Black Lake,
Harvills Hawthorn & Hill Top

Chapel Street residents celebrating the coronation of King George VI and Queen Elizabeth on
12 May 1937. Among the front row: Sylvia Moseley, Maureen Butler, Horace Foster,
Ron Prentice, Freddie Foster, Clara Foster, Dennis Butler, Barbara Worley, Thelma Care,
Alice Prentice, Margaret Grice, Lily Grice. In the crowd behind: Betty Care, Betty Prentice,
Ivy Denham, Thelma Moseley, Beryl Worley, Elsie Wright. (*T.J.H. Price*)

The Roebuck public house at 184 Old Meeting Street, 20 July 1968. Jack Sagar was the licensee here for many years, having previously been landlord of the Royal Exchange at Harvills Hawthorn. Although the pub was demolished many years ago and the terraced houses on the right vacated, it was not until 2002 that these latter properties were also removed. (*Alan Price*)

Old Meeting Street, with Church Lane and the King Edward VII pub on the left, 24 November 1962. A West Bromwich Corporation bus on the No. 75 Wednesbury–Birmingham route is taking on passengers outside the Ebenezer Congregational Chapel. This place of worship, which opened in 1839, closed in 1971 and was registered as a Hindu Shree Krishna temple in 1973. (*David Wilson*)

The Great Western, 74 Chapel Street, 28 June 1960, when Harry Whittingham was the landlord. This Mitchells & Butlers beerhouse was granted a full spirits licence on 3 February 1972, only two years before it closed on 7 April 1974. Joan Elizabeth Massey is on record as the last licensee. (*Andrew Maxam*)

The Sow & Pigs at 26 Hill Top appears to have been two separate buildings judging by the flight of steps leading up to a blank wall in this picture of 20 July 1968, when Jack Horsley was licensee. These premises go back to at least 1801 when landlord John Sheldon, also described as a pig dealer, was living here. (*Alan Price*)

Hill Top from the junction of Coles Lane with the Junior and Infants Council Schools on the right, *c.* 1915. Opposite, behind the second tram standard, is a rare sighting of the Springmakers Arms, which closed in 1961, when Arthur William Williams was the licensee. (*T.J.H. Price*)

The main West Bromwich to Wednesbury road at Hill Top looking towards St James's Church in the distance and Hawkes Lane on the left, *c.* 1915. Paul Barton's post office at 61 Hill Top is the building on the right with three children standing outside. (*T.J.H. Price*)

Landlord Solomon Sheldon (with the walking stick) and his wife pose with customers outside the Stores Inn at Hill Top, *c.* 1900. These premises were de-licensed in 1906 and later taken over by Humphrey Lugg who converted them into an ironmongery store in 1910. Note the 'VR' postbox on the right, which is adjacent to Hill Top post office. (*Lugg Tools Ltd.*)

This picture shows Humphrey Lugg's premises at Hill Top after his conversion of the Stores Inn, a reminder of the pub's name being spelt out above the large double gates. The firm, which was established at 39 Hawkes Lane in 1890, now trades under the name of Lugg Tools Ltd. from new premises at 107 Hill Top. (*Lugg Tools Ltd.*)

Hill Top, looking down Holloway Bank with St James's Church prominent on the right, *c.* 1915. Lord Dartmouth and James Bagnell were the principal subscribers towards the cost of building this church, which was licensed in 1842 and consecrated in 1844. (*Jim Houghton*)

Shops at Hill Top, viewed from the forecourt of St James's Church, May 1962. George Mason opened his grocery premises here around 1922 as did Frank Bratt, whose family butcher's business was previously lower down Hill Top at No. 204. All of these properties were demolished in about 1970 and the Flash Harry pub built on the site. (*T.J.H. Price*)

The Three Crowns, 148 Hill Top, *c.* 1965, when Robert Joseph Williams was the landlord. After Brian Wilkes had pulled the last pint on 28 September 1969 the licence was transferred to the Flash Harry, which opened on 22 April 1971. These new premises were renamed the Hillcrest on 30 November 1979, followed by yet another change in September 1991 to its present-day title The Dovecote. *(Andrew Maxam)*

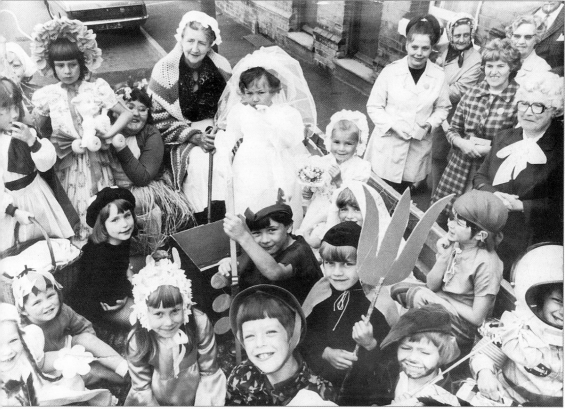

This first parish carnival of St James's Church, Hill Top was opened by Cyrille Regis of West Bromwich Albion at Hateley Heath Infants and Junior School, *c.* 1973. Among those pictured on one of the floats: Judith Dursley (Bo Peep), Catherine Pridmore (grass skirt), Joan Lane (shawl), Paula Tandy (bride), Emma Neadle (bridesmaid), Jamie Neadle (Robin Hood), Lee Hill (Lucifer). Bottom centre: Judith Howells, Paul Humpherson. (*St James's Church*)

The Globe Inn, 89 Holloway Bank, Hill Top, 20 September 1962. George Jones, the licensee at the time took over these premises on 7 January 1943 and remained here for the next twenty years, handing over to John Harris on 26 September 1963. Mitchells & Butlers acquired the Highgate Walsall Brewery Co. in 1939 and were themselves subsumed by Bass in 1967. The pub closed on 7 October 1973, with Edward Jackson being the last licensee. (*Andrew Maxam*)

Ellen and Florence Johnson are pictured here standing in the doorway of their grocery shop at 181 Hill Top, *c.* 1938. These premises closed, and were demolished, around 1952, having been in the Johnson family's possession since 1922. (*T.J.H. Price*)

A rare picture, taken in about 1898, of a steam tram passing over the River Tame Bridge at the foot of Holloway Bank, Hill Top, which divides the two parishes of Wednesbury and West Bromwich. Wednesbury Bridge, or Finchpath Bridge as it was known in the sixteenth century, was rebuilt by Thomas Telford in 1826 as part of his improvements to Holyhead Road. (*T.J.H. Price*)

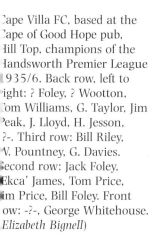

Cape Villa FC, based at the Cape of Good Hope pub, Hill Top, champions of the Handsworth Premier League 1935/6. Back row, left to right: ? Foley, ? Wootton, Tom Williams, G. Taylor, Jim Peak, J. Lloyd, H. Jesson, ?-. Third row: Bill Riley, W. Pountney, G. Davies. Second row: Jack Foley, 'Ekca' James, Tom Price, Jim Price, Bill Foley. Front row: -?-, George Whitehouse. *Elizabeth Bignell*)

Price's fish and chip shop and the British Oak pub, Hawkes Lane, Hill Top, 13 July 1968. Joan Whiting, the pub's licensee, had been here only two and a half years before it closed on 21 September 1969. Virtually the whole of this lane, including Jonah Wright's scrapyard, has since become a housing development. (*Alan Price*)

The extensive premises of the White Swan Inn, 69 Hawkes Lane, on the corner of Hill Street, *c.* 1904. With so many public houses in Hawkes Lane and the surrounding area, it is hardly surprising that this establishment closed down during the First World War. By 1920, however, it had become a hardware store run by Mrs Annette Wooldridge. (*Alan Price*)

William John Evans looks out from the doorway of the Globe Inn at 46 New Street, Hill Top, *c.* 1936. The beer was supplied by Samuel Woodhall's brewery, which was taken over by Julia Hanson & Sons of Dudley in 1937. George Cope has the record for longevity here after holding the licence from 5 October 1939 until 28 July 1966. Amos Harper is standing fourth from the right. (*Dorothy Burton*)

Hill Top British Legion annual dinner, *c.* 1925. The vicar of St James's Church, William B. Houldey, is standing left of centre at the back. Second and fourth from the left: Joseph Birch, William K. Harper, comedian and compère. These headquarters pre-date those which were situated at the junction of Hawkes Lane and New Street known as 'The Mustard Gas Hospital'. (*Joyce Partridge*)

Hill Top Wesleyan Methodist Chapel, Harvills Hawthorn, *c.* 1920. The chapel was built in 1850, replacing an older structure dating from 1830. It had 1,000 sittings but by about 1940 numbers had declined and services were being held in the Sunday School. The present Methodist Church in New Street, Hill Top, was opened in 1955. (*T.J.H. Price*)

The 6th West Bromwich Company Boys Brigade, attached to Hill Top Methodist Church, pictured at Tiddington, Stratford upon Avon, *c.* 1945. Back row, left to right: Alf Smith, -?-, Brian Bunch, Ernie Wood, Fred Hodges, -?-, Bill Baker, Ken Bissell. Front row: Colin Snape, Barry Osell, Derek Easthope, -?-, -?-, -?-, -?-. (*Ken Bissell*)

Hill Top Methodist Church Sunday School Anniversary, *c.* 1950. The Revd Clifford Hunt is pictured in the centre of this group with Mr Hancox to the right. Other members of the congregation are from left to right: Ray Maddox, Margaret Kerr, Jean Connah, Harold Beaseley, ? Edwards, Len Hubbard, -?-, Joan Legg, -?-, Winnie Beaseley, -?-, Gladys Hubbard, Doris Hancox. (*Mary Reynolds*)

Members of Hill Top Methodist Church attending the Christmas morning service, 1969. Back row, left to right: Stan Adcock, Ben Maddox, Michael ?, Paul Reynolds, Norman Reynolds, -?-, Margaret Adcock, -?-. Middle row: Janet Edwards, Carol Hipkiss, Alice Marsters, Mary Reynolds, Winnie Beaseley, -?-, -?-, Helen Adcock, ? Hodgetts, ? Day, Karen Adcock. Front row, left: Arthur Bailey, Stephen Maddox, Ray Maddox, Olive Maddox. (*Mary Reynolds*)

The Hawthorn Tavern, 245 Dial Lane, Harvills Hawthorn, *c.* 1930. Harry Jones had been the landlord here since the First World War and was also the first in the new pub which replaced it around 1938. These latter premises were modernised in 1969 at a cost of £20,000, when Waclaw Tarkowski was licensee, with further structural alterations taking place in June 1989. Although the pub is still open it must hold the record for numbers of previous licensees, no less than forty-five since 1965! The old Hawthorn Tavern pictured here dates from around 1800 when the highway in front of it was known as Brickhouse Lane. An early licensee, John Gittoes, was also described in Kelly's Trade Directory of 1845 as a farmer, which shows how rural the area must have been at that time. (*Keith Hodgkins*)

Residents of Wolesley Road, Harvills Hawthorn, pictured celebrating the coronation of Queen Elizabeth II on 2 June 1953. Among the front row, left to right: Gordon Stevens, Desmond Bull, Brian Newell, Ian Dawson, Christine Smith, Walter Ford, Carol Ford, Josie Dawson, Pat Bradley, Tommy Bromley, Bernadette Bromley, Glynis Smith, Madeline Reece. Those behind: Charlie Bromley, Doris Bromley, Royston Haynes, Doris Smith, Ernie Smith, John Edmunds, Jack Edmunds, Peter Phillips, Beattie Lawley, Dot Parry, Frank Parry, Lyn Parry (*Shirley Mauldridge*)

Harvills Hawthorn from the junction of Hawkes Lane and New Street, 13 July 1968, with, on the corner of Peter Street (left), the Samson & Lion public house managed by William Andrew Davies. It was originally owned by Bents Brewery Co. Ltd of Liverpool before eventually becoming a Bass and then a Manns house on 16 May 1980. During the 1990s this building was structurally altered and made into two retail outlets one of which became an off-licence on 15 July 1997. (*Alan Price*)

Almost the same view of Harvills Hawthorn as the above picture, but this one was taken fifty years earlier, in 1918. During this period the only noticeable changes that have taken place are from Dial Lane on the left down toward Golds Hill in the distance. (*Ken Rock*)

A winter view of the Miners Arms, 58 Bagnall Street, Golds Hill, when Ann Fletcher was the licensee, 1956. Note the old houses on the left occupying the future site of the Warwick Rim & Sectioning's new building. (*Andrew Maxam*)

Golds Green Methodist Chapel Sunday School Anniversary, *c.* 1963. Back row, left to right: Geoff Cooper, Norman Reynolds (organist). Sixth row: John Bailey, Tom Taylor, Michael Cooper, -?-, Judith Rolfe, Pa? Bailey, -?-, Christine Bailey, Eric Reynolds, Jack Cartwright, Stan Barnes. Fifth row: Joan Faulkner, Jean Humphries, Susan Haywood, Lily Rolfe, Christine Rolfe, Joan Hill, ? Glendenning, Jean Westwood, Mavi? Glendenning, Doris Glendenning, Polly Bennett, Elsie Price, Sally Davies. Among those in the centre section? Linda Reynolds, Anita Price, Ann Reynolds, Kevin Cooper, Richard Bailey. (*Mary Reynolds*)

The bar of the Spring Cottage, 155 Harvills Hawthorn, 1954, where Joseph Butler is celebrating his retirement after thirty years as licensee. This pub, better known as 'Joe Butler's', closed on 4 October 1961. Among the back row: Joe Roberts, Lily Walker, ? Highfield, Harold Whitehouse, Ray Homer. Middle section: Lily Daniels, Joe Butler Jnr., Albert Parkes, Hilda Butler, Arthur Reed. Front row: -?-, Joseph Butler, Elizabeth Butler, Joan Butler, Marjorie Butler, Richard Taylor. (*Lily Phillips*)

The Old Crown FC, Division 2 members of the West Bromwich Sunday League, *c.* 1969. Back row, left to right: Graham Bennett, Ken Law, Tom Hughes, Ernie Hughes, Colin Male, Philip Clift, John Garbett, George Poynton Snr. Front row: Alan Hughes, Brian Richardson, George Poynton Jnr, Terry Mansell, David ?, Billy Hughes. (*Ernie Hughes*)

A 'King Class' locomotive 4–6–0, No. 6001 *King Edward VII*, hauling a passenger train, emerges from Hill Top tunnel heading north towards Wednesbury on 27 June 1961, with houses alongside Tunnel Road shown in the background. This line now carries the Birmingham–Wolverhampton Midland Metro tramway system, which opened on 30 May 1999. (*David Williams*)

Ratcliffs (GB) Ltd, Golds Hill, works outing to Amsterdam by Transair Airlines, 15–16 June 1956. Among those in front of the plane, from left to right: Arthur Curtis, Tommy Lloyd, Fred Cooksey, ? Fenton-Smith, Jean Turner, Sylvia Harris, Olive Holtom, Josie Phipps, Albert Sadler, Horace Smith, Dick Attwood, Sid Webb, Bill Tansley. (*Betty Johnson*)

Chapter Four

Great Barr, Lyndon & Tantany

The original Maltshovel Inn, Newton Road, Great Barr, *c.* 1902, where Thomas Marsh the proprietor is advertising home-brewed ales, produced no doubt in the adjoining barn. Asbury Cottage, the boyhood home of Francis Asbury, who in 1771 became an apostle of Methodism in America, is located at the rear of this inn. The cottage was purchased by the borough in 1955 and after restoration was reopened and dedicated on Friday 27 November 1959.
(*T.J.H. Price*)

The Scott Bridge (High Bridges), Newton Road, Great Barr, *c.* 1930. This rural scene also shows the rear of houses numbered 174–80, adjacent to the Tame Valley Canal which was opened on 14 February 1844. The bridge pictured here was reconstructed between 1967 and 1969 and officially opened by Cllr S.J. Bryant on 23 January 1970. (*T.J.H. Price*)

The crossroads at Scott Arms from Queslett Road, *c.* 1930. Newton Road is directly ahead with Walsall Road to the left and Birmingham Road right. The Scott Arms (left), built in 1786 as a coaching inn, eventually became a victim of the demolition men in 1966 when the surrounding area was redeveloped and the road widened. (*Anthony Page*)

This remarkable picture of Newton Road, Great Barr, *c.* 1910, shows the Scott Arms crossroads up ahead with Queslett Road in the distance. On the right corner is the rear of the Scott Arms public house, which was replaced in 1968 with new premises built further back from the road. (*T.J.H. Price*)

Children in Appleton Avenue, Great Barr pictured prior to a coach tour of Birmingham during the Queen Elizabeth II coronation celebrations of 2 June 1953. Front row, left to right: Raymond Coley, -?-, Terry Coley, Andrew Bird, Paul Gibbard, -?-, -?-, Lyndon Laney, Richard Powell, Marlene Bull, -?-, Paul Whitehouse, -?-, Judith Haines, -?-, Pauline Hill, Among those behind: David Powell, Lee Sharman, Rita Baker. (*Kathleen Powell*)

Birmingham Road, Great Barr, with Pages Lane in the distance on the left, *c.* 1910. It is hard to believe that this is the same route used by motorists today when approaching junction 7 of the M6 motorway. (*T.J.H. Price*)

Fancy dress paraders outside 26 Appleton Avenue, Great Barr on the occasion of Queen Elizabeth II coronation, 2 June 1953. Back row, left to right: Diane Brookes, Pauline Russell, Marlene Bull, Christine Ashmore, Hazel Drake, Paul Whitehouse, -?-, Ken Davies, Pauline Wedgbury, Rita Baker, -?-, Bob Frost, Susan Bird, Andrew Bird, John Russell, -?-. Front row: Lyndon Laney, Richard Powell, Gloria Holland, Alma ?, Majorie Titchener, -?-, -?-, Lee Sharman, Verlain Badderley, Paul Gibbard, Andrea Fitzpatrick, Terry Ashmore, Barry Wedgbury. (*Edith Davies*)

Railway Terrace and the Beaufort Arms Hotel, Old Walsall Road, Hamstead, *c*. 1910. The border with Birmingham, which now runs along this road, was redrawn in 1928 when 645 acres of land at Hamstead were added to West Bromwich from the urban district of Perry Barr. (*Anthony Page*)

Hamstead miners' wives and children's outing to New Brighton, *c*. 1948. Back row, left to right: ? Hibbetts, ? Bland, ? Smith, ? Smith, -?-, ? Smith, Barbara Bland, ? Connop, ? Connop, Audrey Bradbury, ? Timmins, Liz Leatherland, ? Bradbury, ? Timmins, Lily Clements, -?-, ? Williams, Harold Beaumont, George Leatherland, ? Jones, ? Stevens, Irene Beaumont, -?-, ? Stevens, ? Stevens. Among the front row: Alan Leatherland, Fred Timmins, Keith Jones, Hazel Timmins. (*Harold Beaumont*)

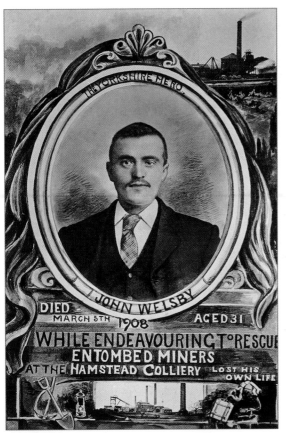

John Welsby, the Yorkshire hero of the Hamstead Colliery disaster of Wednesday 4 March 1908 portrayed here on one of a series of postcards published by W. Gothard of Barnsley. Twenty-four miners and one member of the Barnsley rescue team, John Welsby, died as a result of this tragedy. Following the inquest into Welsby's death, which was held at the nearby Beaufort Arms public house, questions were inevitably asked as to why there were no rescue teams other than those which travelled all the way down from Yorkshire. The home secretary at the time, W.E. Gladstone, replied by stating that there were only two places in England, namely Barnsley and Normanton, where specialist breathing apparatus and men trained to use it were available. A relief fund was afterwards set up which raised a total of £11,794 9s 9d, with HM King Edward VII donating 150 guineas and Queen Alexandra £100. On Monday 6 July 1908 the mayor of Birmingham presented gold and silver medals to forty men who had been involved in the rescue attempts, including a special presentation to John Welsby's widow. In 1971, as a tribute to his heroic attempt to reach the trapped miners, Welsby Avenue in Hamstead was named after him by West Bromwich council. (*T.J.H. Price*)

The Hamstead public house, 89 Green Lane, Hamstead, March 1961. This was originally a fine private residence standing in its own grounds before being granted a licence to sell ale. Francis James Nash held the licence here for almost twenty-four years from 22 April 1965. When this picture was taken, however, John Thomas Dunn was in charge. (*Sidney Darby*)

The Royal Oak, 14 Newton Street, 20 May 1982, when William Raymond Tiler was the licensee. This pub dates from about 1860, when a trade directory records Joseph Oakley as the landlord. Before this, according to John Wood's map of 1837, fields were the dominant feature of this area, with no buildings or streets shown. The nearest beerhouse was the Ring of Bells, All Saints' Street, in the centre of Churchfields. (*T.J.H. Price*)

Licensees of the Royal Oak, Newton Street, Ted and Alice England are shown here being presented with gifts from customers to mark their retirement from the licensing trade on 7 January 1971. Front row, left to right: Alice England, Tommy Westwood, Ted England. Among those in the bar: Tony Usherwood, Basil Penny, Jimmy Evans, Alan Machin, Vic Faulkner, Ray Mountford, Stan Green, Derek Penn, Archie Parsons, Margaret Pace, Ernie Brierley, Jim Ralley, Cynthia Ralley. (*Iris Brown*)

All Saints' Church, also known as 'the Old Church', viewed from the entrance to Heath Lane, *c.* 1930. The name All Saints' is relatively new since before the nineteenth century this church was known as St Clement's. A lane bearing this title near Lyndon reminds us of the fact. (*T.J.H. Price*)

The Hall End Tavern at 99 Church Lane, (later renamed Vicarage Road), *c.* 1904. These premises were replaced in the 1930s by the modern present-day building, with Jimmy James becoming its first licensee. Left to right: Tom Deamer, Ellen Horton Deamer, Henry Horton (licensee), Elsie Horton, Herbert Horton. (*T.J.H. Price*)

The Ring of Bells, 87 All Saints' Street, Churchfields, *c.* 1905. Dating from about 1800, this pub was well known for having a 'pound' in the front of it where stray horses could be locked up until they were claimed by their owners. As a result, it became known throughout the Black Country as 'the pub that sells beer by the pound'! It was demolished for road widening in 1971, C.W. Webb being the last licensee. (*T.J.H. Price*)

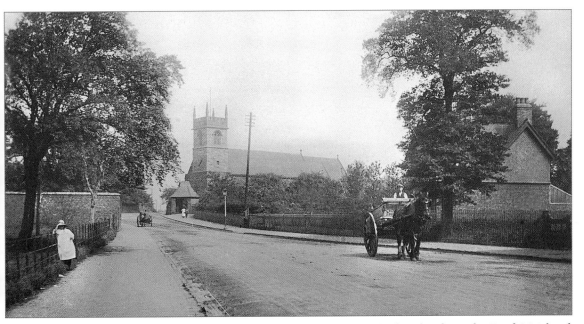

An idyllic scene at Churchfields, *c.* 1908, looking towards All Saints' Church where the Revd Muirhead Mitchell Conner MA was the vicar and rural dean. The rural nature of this area is apparent by what looks like a local farmer in his horse and cart heading towards the Ring of Bells pub. (*T.J.H. Price*)

'Sots Hole' at Church Vale, with, top right, Hill House Farm, a timbered sixteenth-century building with later additions of brick, *c.* 1910. Charles Dickens is reputed to have stayed at Hill House while writing *The Old Curiosity Shop*. It was also the home of Captain James Eaton RN, who served with Nelson during the Battle of Trafalgar. He died here in 1857 and is buried in All Saints' Church graveyard. (*T.J.H. Price*)

Charles Dixon's newsagent premises at 165–7 Hargate Lane, on the corner of Grafton Road, 1944. The shop also sold groceries and tobacco, but the window display here is showing photographs of local servicemen as part of a National Savings 'Salute the Soldier' week during the Second World War. (*Anita Warner*)

The junction of Hallam and Lewisham Streets during visiting hours at Hallam Hospital, *c.* 1930. Previously known as 'the Infirmary' it was looked on with a degree of disdain by some locals because of the hospital's former association with the Union Workhouse situated within its grounds. (*T.J.H. Price*)

Field Marshal Montgomery ('Monty') prepares to leave Hallam Hospital during 1944 after visiting Military Ward Three, where troops wounded in the Second World War were being treated. He is just visible behind the windscreen of the first car parked in the driveway leading to Lewisham Street. (*Mary Quigley*)

Bakery workers of Messrs J.J. & P.L. Grant Ltd. outside the firm's original premises in Taylors Lane, June 1928. Percival Grant founded the business in about 1915 in the shop pictured left of the group and, judging by the new brickwork, probably added the bakery to it himself. One of their employees, Susan May Stevens, is standing fifth from the right. (*Joyce Brown*)

The Five Ways Inn (The Fourpenny Shop) and the Hare & Hounds Inn, 58 and 60 Seagar Street, *c.* 1982, when Thomas Forrester and Ernest Anderson were the licensees. The Hare & Hounds was apparently the headquarters of a notorious forger during the early 1800s named William Booth, who was hanged for his crimes at Stafford Assizes on 15 August 1812. This pub closed on 3 October 1991 when it merged with the Five Ways Inn to become a single licensed premises. (*T.J.H. Price*)

Frederick Green (left), the landlord of the Horse & Jockey, Stoney Lane, and his wife Kathleen (right), line up to be photographed with their customers, *c.* 1914. This Banks's pub is still going strong with the present clientele looking somewhat different to these characters. (*Patrick Green*)

Woodward Street, decorated for the coronation of Queen Elizabeth II, June 1953. The corner building on the right was a mission chapel, built in 1880–1, and belonged to Mayers Green Church. Known locally as Woodward Street Mission, it was bought by West Bromwich Corporation under a compulsory purchase order in 1969. (*T.J.H. Price*)

The Crown Inn, 1 Mill Street, corner of Hargate Lane, 8 June 1968, where Thomas Edward Mansell was 'mine host'. One of two 'Crowns' in the area, this one had an outstanding record when it came to long-serving landlords: Ernest Hadley from 1918 to 6 October 1938, and Charles Sumner from 1938 to 3 January 1963, were exceptional. It closed on 8 January 1979 with Yvonne Lillian Farley as the last licensee. (*Andrew Maxam*)

The Boot & Slipper, 114 Sandwell Road, near to Beale Street, *c.* 1951. Thomas Stanley Inkson is seen standing in the doorway of this Butlers house where he was licensee from 29 September 1949 until 25 October 1951. Only one more landlord would follow before James Smith became the last prior to the pub's closure on 15 April 1958. (*Bill Inkson*)

John W. Bird's confectionery, newsagents and stationers shop on the corner of New Street and Seagar Street, *c.* 1926. New Street on the left had been extended between Walsall Street and the main Dartmouth Park entrance a few years earlier, sweeping away old properties in the Four Acres and Mayers Green areas. (*Iris Reynolds*)

Park Crescent, off Seagar Street, *c.* 1926. This small housing development was built on the site of the Four Acres football and cricket ground which, between 1882 and 1885, was the home of West Bromwich Albion FC. Albion's biggest match here was against Blackburn Rovers in the FA Cup on 21 February 1885 when a crowd of 16,393 saw the 'Baggies' lose 0–2. (*T.J.H. Price*)

Pigeon flying has always been a great Black Country sport with a following today just as strong as in yesteryear. This picture shows a typical loft of about 1900, situated in the back yard of 20 Temple Street. These prize-winning birds belonged to Mathias Wheatley, on the left, and Edward Wheatley, right. (*Beattie Thompson*)

The Church Tavern, 1 Sandwell Road, when William Andrew Davies was licensee, 12 October 1959. Although it had quite an impressive frontage, the status was that of a beerhouse until 1950 when a full licence to serve wines and spirits was obtained. Albert Booker was the pub's landlord when it closed on 7 October 1969. On the right are the premises of Spencers, wine and spirit merchants. (*Jim Houghton*)

Judging by the absence of ladies in these two charabancs, it is fairly certain that this was a Sunday morning breakfast run, *c.* 1920, from the Old Crown, 56 Sandwell Road, which is pictured in the background. Landlord John Paddock is probably in one of the coaches, which were on hire from Noah Turner's Sandwell Garage in New Street. (*Lou Reed*)

A parade, possibly by members of the home guard, photographed in Sandwell Road on 15 November 1941. By coincidence the Sandwell Cinema has also been captured by the photographer, making this the only known picture of it to exist. The building started out as a Baptist Chapel in 1812 but went into decline, opening as a cinema on 24 August 1922. (*Lou Reed*)

Tantany suffered considerably from enemy bombing during the Second World War. This picture shows a crater at the junction of Shaftesbury and Law Streets on the morning of 11 November 1940, following an air raid the previous evening. (*South Staffs Water*)

Queen Elizabeth II coronation celebrations in Nelson Street, 2 June 1953. Back row, left to right: Gwen Love, Nancy Love, ? Lloyd, Edna Lloyd, Violet Parsons, Leah Parsons, ? Grice, -?-, Joseph Dexter, ? Parsons, -?-, Clifford Round, ? Parsons. Middle section: Marlene Phillips, Rita Brookes, Gladys Blakemore, James Dexter, Eileen Brookes, Jean Winston, Eric Lloyd, Clifford Lloyd, Eileen Winston, Joan Love, Pearl Love, Brenda Love, Ruth Deatheridge, Frances Gould, Violet Yates, Geoff Parsons, Margaret Phillips, Emma Dexter, Valerie Yates, Margaret Yates. Front row: Flossie Bromley, Florrie Gould, Michael Brookes. (*T.J.H. Price*)

Second World War bomb damage in Haigh Street, Tantany, the morning following an enemy air raid on 10 November 1940. Sewage and other water facilities were severely affected but normal service was restored by the South Staffordshire Water Company within a few days. (*South Staffs Water*)

The Windmill Inn, 18 Tantany Lane, March 1961, where James William Norris was the landlord. The pub takes its name from a windmill which once stood near the junction of Mill Street and Tantany Lane. After the inn's closure on 30 November 1969, when Elsie Cartwright was the landlady, it had been intended to transfer the licence to proposed new premises on the corner of Wellington Street which would have been known as the Red Robin, but nothing came of it. (*Sidney Darby*)

Frederick Lewis Hodge's confectionery and general store, 197 Walsall Street, *c.* 1930. Frederick, who had previously worked at Jubilee Colliery, opened this shop in 1926 just after his marriage to Laura Annie Ford. Soon afterwards the business became a partnership with Laura's sister Nellie and her husband Jim Andrews, but it was not to last long. By 1930 Fred and Laura had withdrawn from the arrangement and moved to Great Bridge where they opened another confectionery shop, next door to Herbert Smith the fishmonger. Their Great Bridge premises also included billiard tables situated in rooms at the rear which proved very popular with the locals, but by 1938 a decision had been made to sell the business. Meanwhile, back in Walsall Street, Nellie and Jim had given up their shop shortly after the departure of Fred and Laura in 1930. Laura's sister Nellie can be seen on this photograph, taken outside the Walsall Street shop, standing in the doorway with her daughter Nora by her side. (*Keith Hodgkins*)

Charles Henry Griffiths was the landlord when this picture of the Hargate Tavern, 123 Hargate Lane, was taken on 19 April 1960, and he was still there when it closed on 25 October 1970. This was another of those beerhouses which was noted for the stability of its licensees, with Thomas Moorhouse staying for over thirty years before the 1940s. (*Andrew Maxam*)

Chapter Five

Charlemont, Stone Cross & Yew Tree

Committee members of Charlemont Social Club and Institute preparing bread rolls for the ox roast in celebration of King George V and Queen Mary's Silver Jubilee, 6 May 1935. The ox was supplied by local butcher Howard Hughes of Hollyhedge Road, who is on the left in a long white coat. Standing next to him wearing a bowler hat is Bill Scholey.
(Carol Osborne)

The ox roast taking place on land adjoining Charlemont Social Club and Institute, 6 May 1935. Hundreds of people turned out for this event, which must have created quite a stir in the surrounding area. Even the local 'bobby' was there, behind the men in white coats. (*Carol Osborne*)

Charlemont Shopping Centre, Hollyhedge Road, *c.* 1935. Only four of these retail outlets are still operating in the same line of business as when this picture was taken. R & J Stores was originally Harry Maplethorpe, grocer and post office; the present-day greengrocer's at No. 112 and drapers at No. 116 were owned by Benjamin Peakman and Mary Evans respectively, the Stars News Shop started out as William Hogan's newsagent; and Elsie Mountain's fried fish shop at No. 124 is now Mario's Fish Bar. (*T.J.H. Price*)

Pennyhill Lane, Charlemont, looking towards Hollyhedge Road, *c.* 1932. 'Pennyhill' is a Danish place-name derived from a Scandinavian word, which in its original form was spelt *knapenny*, 'knap' signifying a bare hill. No. 32 is the first house on the right, with the remainder in descending order. (*T.J.H. Price*)

The 14th West Bromwich Company Boys Brigade from Charlemont Methodist Church at their annual camp, Whitecliff Bay, Isle of Wight, *c.* 1964. Back row, left to right: Philip Dixon, -?-, Martin ?, Ian Jordan, ? Cook, Christopher Hawkins, Brian Stubbs, -?-. Third row: Ken Bissell, Paul Tedstone, David Timmins, Andrew Alldritt, Graham Sneddon, Kelvin Alldritt, Christopher Bissell, John Stubbs, Don Evans. Second row: Les While, Frank Cook, Mary Bissell, Linda Cook, Christine Evans, Vera Evans, Lillian Cook, Dorothy While, -?-, 'Grandad' Reeves. Front row: Paul Dickens, -?-, -?-, David While, Paul While, -?-, Alan Gould, David Payne. (*Ken Bissell*)

Page's Bungalow Stores, on the corner of Charlemont Road and Hollyhedge Road, *c.* 1932. The proprietor B.C. Page in the white apron, published a number of these high quality postcard views of the Charlemont area soon after it was built up, including this one of his stores. These premises, which once sold grocery and newspapers, have since been converted into a private residence. (*T.J.H. Price*)

One of Page's views of Bustleholme Lane, Charlemont, *c.* 1932, looking north towards what in recent years has become Whitworth Drive. The houses seen here, from right to left, start at 91 and increase in numerical order. The skyline pictured at the end of this lane is now completely obscured by tree growth. (*T.J.H. Price*)

Beyond the trees in the centre of this photograph from about 1932 is the rooftop of Charlemont Farm, which at this time stood within an area of 54 acres. It was let to farmer Walter Wilkes on an annual tenancy at the rent of £100 per year by Henry Dawes, a veterinary surgeon. Charlemont Bowling Club now occupies this site, although the house pictured left is still there. (*T.J.H. Price*)

Charlemont Methodist Church Primary and Beginners Sunday School Anniversary, June 1981. Among the back row: Carol Redpath, Kay Anderson. Third row: Julia Mason, Emma Makepeace, Donna Makepeace, Lynsey Webb. Second row: Nicola Harper, Mark Hiley. Front row: Steven ?, -?-, -?-, Emma Mark, -?-, -?-, Ben Mark, Jason Wheeler. Conducting the children, on the right: David Payne. (*David Woodman*)

The base of the original seventeenth-century wayside stone cross in Hall Green Road is still visible in this picture from about 1890. A representation of this cross was unveiled near the site in December 2002, but it bears little resemblance to the four-way finger post shown here. In the background Ann Martin stands in the doorway of the Stone Cross Inn where her husband William is licensee. (*T.J.H. Price*)

A replacement for the old sandstone cross was erected in 1897 at the junction of Hall Green Road and Walsall Road, on the top of which was fitted a gas lantern. This view from about 1932 shows its vandalised state after each of the pointers had gradually disappeared over the preceding thirty-five years. A number of pictures taken over this period show the cross with four, three or no pointers at all. (*T.J.H. Price*)

Hall Green Road from Walsall Road, Stone Cross, *c. 1935*. The small building between the houses on the left was the premises of Albert Franks & Sons who were electrical engineers before taking over Charlemont Motor Garage, Walsall Road in 1938. They moved to their present Spon Lane location in 1969 and are now trading under the name of Sandwell Garages Ltd, a main Vauxhall dealership. (*T.J.H. Price*)

The Stone Cross, 140 Walsall Road, *c. 1968*. These replacement premises opened in 1935 when Albert Edgar Woodward was landlord, having succeeded Thomas Snead at the inn's previous location in 1921. In 1951, after completing thirty years at these two pubs, Albert retired, handing over the tenancy to Albert Edward Kirkham. Five years later in February 1956 Albert Woodward's son Ted obtained the licence which he held for a record twenty-four years until his retirement from the trade on 9 October 1980. (*Andrew Maxam*)

Bungalows numbered 72 to 78 Charlemont Road, Bird End are seen in this rural view published by B.C. Page, *c.* 1932. The fields in the background now contain part of the M5/M6 motorway interchange, which opened in 1970. (*T.J.H. Price*)

Temporary supports being fitted at Stone Cross Colliery to 18-inch and 24-inch water mains in Walsall Road, between Marsh Lane and Hall Green Road, July 1920. The colliery was owned at this time by the Brierley Colliery Company. South Staffs Water took these measures to prevent any sudden fracture of the pipes as a result of coal mining excavations in this area. Just visible in the distance is the old Stone Cross Inn. (*South Staffs Water*)

Walsall Road from the Navigation canal bridge, 18 April 1964. The Navigation Inn, on the right, closed on 20 July 1998 and was subsequently replaced with a private housing development. To the left is the spot where, on 6 February 1962, a chemical lorry exploded which afterwards necessitated the demolition of six houses, with thirty more needing major repairs. (*David Wilson*)

West Bromwich Boys Club FC, members of the Walsall Minor League, January 1959. Back row, left to right: Jim Payne, Doug Smith, Brian Markham, Brian Griffiths, John Bates, Danny Mills, Tony Brierley, David Thompson. Front row: Billy Jones, Trevor Roberts, Alan Sheppard, John Sheppard, Ken Gadd. (*Brian Markham*)

The Friar Park Inn, better known as 'The Cabin', 103 Crankhall Lane, March 1961, during Joseph Henry Bailey's tenancy. Although having a Wednesbury postal address this is in fact a West Bromwich pub, which until 1929 was called the Canal Tavern. The adjacent Friar Park council estate was built by West Bromwich Corporation around 1930. (*T.J.H. Price*)

Walsall Road from the River Tame Bridge looking towards the Bulls Head in the centre of the picture, *c.* 1908. In 1931 this area was part of 332 acres transferred from the parish of Wednesbury to West Bromwich, with a small parcel of land at Bescot going to Walsall. The Bescot railway station and marshalling yards however, remained within the borders of West Bromwich. (*T.J.H. Price*)

This area of the Walsall Road near the Navigation Inn appears to have had more than its fair share of disasters with this one the result of an air raid during the Second World War. The date of this picture is 10 April 1941, and according to local people German bombers had been attempting to destroy the nearby Bescot Railway Marshalling Yards the previous evening. (*South Staffs Water*)

Bescot Railway Marshalling Yards can be seen on the left in this picture of Walsall Road, taken on 12 April 1964. A No. 2 Bus on the Great Bridge–Yew Tree Estate route is just passing the Bulls Head on the right, which was demolished around 1969 when the M6 motorway came through here. (*David Wilson*)

The Archers, Thorncroft Way, Yew Tree Estate, April 1962. These premises were opened on 29 July 1955 with Harold Gillard being one of the early licensees. Following major refurbishment, a few years ago the name was initially changed to The Sadlers, but after an outcry from the customers who were fans of West Bromwich Albion the pub was quickly renamed The Orchard. (*Andrew Maxam*)

Members of the Yew Tree Methodist Church Youth Club check their route in preparation for a sponsored walk in aid of church funds, *c.* 1968. Among the front row: John Bunyard, Christine Pearce, Susanne Withers. Standing behind: Tony Gibbard, Jim Jones, Malcolm Dyke, Barbara Bateman, Leslie Dyke, Pam Hodgetts, Janet Fellows, Malcom Hopkins. Holding the map is Harry Collins and at the back wearing a cap, David Dyke. (*Harry Collins*)

The 10th West Bromwich Boys Brigade (attached to Yew Tree Methodist Church) awards evening, *c.* 1962. Making the presentations was Cllr Minnie Evitts, Mayor of West Bromwich. Among the back row: Keith Brookes. Third row: Jim Jones, Edwin Bowles, Cllr Minnie Evitts, Harry Collins, George Spencer, Malcolm Hopkins. Front row: George Wood, Robert Spencer, Derek Pointon. (*Jim Jones*)

A ladies' outing to Josiah Wedgwood & Sons Ltd, Stoke on Trent, from Yew Tree Methodist Church, *c.* 1965. Back row, left to right: Celia Edey, Doris Boffy, Clara Whitehouse. Fourth row: Florrie Pointon, Ada Dyke, Mary Nightingale, Vera Bricknell, -?-, -?-. Among the third row: Annie Jackson, Winifred Baker. Second row: Gladys Taylor. Front row: -?-, Agness Collins, ? Wilkes, Gwenda Withers, -?-, -?-, -?-. (*Ada Dyke*)

Over 200 senior citizens were treated to a dinner at the Yew Tree Social & Labour Club on 25 May 1966, the cost being met by the membership and donations from local firms. Pictured between the tables are the Mayor and Mayoress of West Bromwich, Cllr Joshua Churchman and his wife Violet. (*Joshua Churchman*)

Around 200 senior citizens from the Yew Tree Estate enjoyed the opera *Trial by Jury*, when members of the Mount Operatic Society from Walsall entertained them at their annual party on 25 January 1967. Later, the Mayor and Mayoress of West Bromwich, Cllr Joshua Churchman and his wife Violet, presented around fifty food parcels to winners in a competition. (*Joshua Churchman*)

Chapter Six
Schooldays

Rita Hallard, first year junior teacher at Fisher Street School, Great Bridge, demonstrates the Cuisenaire method of learning mathematics. Each coloured rod represented a number and was so named after Emil Georges Cuisenaire (1891–1976), a Belgian educationalist. Margaret Aston is the fourth child from the left. (*Rita Hallard*)

Black Lake Junior and Infants School physical training class, *c.* 1957. These premises opened in 1885 as a Mixed and Infants Board School changing to separate boys, girls and infants in 1918. Alan Hunt is standing in front of the left window at the back, while Alan Gardner and Philip Hopkins are front and rear of the vaulting-horse. (*Alan Hunt*)

A mixed physical training class at Black Lake Junior and Infants School, *c.* 1957. After reverting back to a mixed school in 1943 it continued as such until closure occurred in 1969. Alan Hunt and Peter Fellows are standing below the left window at the back. (*Alan Hunt*)

The presentation by Cllr Joshua Churchman JP, Mayor of West Bromwich, of a certificate marking Black Lake Infants and Junior School's fifty-year membership of the National Savings movement, 7 October 1966. On his left is headmistress Mrs P.E. Phelps, with Assistant District Commissioner for National Savings, A.B.H. Asslin, to his right. (*Joshua Churchman*)

Hill Top School FC, undefeated winners of the inter-schools Trophy, 1949. Back row, left to right: Jack Reynolds, Alan Taylor, Billy Foster, Frank Billington, Leslie Jones, Brian Bunce, ? Lewis (headmaster). Front row: George Pritchard, George Worton, Brian Waite, Arthur Gibson, Eric Smith, Ron Evans, Tom Edwards, Gilbert Boxley. (*George Pritchard*)

George Salter Secondary Modern Boys School Science Club, *c.* 1949. Back row, left to right: -?-, -?-, Alan Partridge, George Barnett, -?-, Patrick Law, Alan Broomhall, -?-, -?-, Freddy Fletcher, -?-. Middle row: Frank Roberts, -?-, -?-, Ray Whale, ? Jacobs, Arthur Mills, ? Appleton, -?-, -?-. Front row: Raymond Angel, Brian Rayers, Alan Toovey, -?-, Brian Wheatley, Eddie Slater, Robert Bullock, Reg Price, -?-, John Baker. (*Brian Rayers*)

George Salter Secondary Boys School Basketball Team, 1960/1. Back row, left to right: Alan Doggett, John Garbett. Front row: Geoff Roper, Jim Gittins, Brian Walford, Jimmy Ridgeway. (*Alan Doggett*)

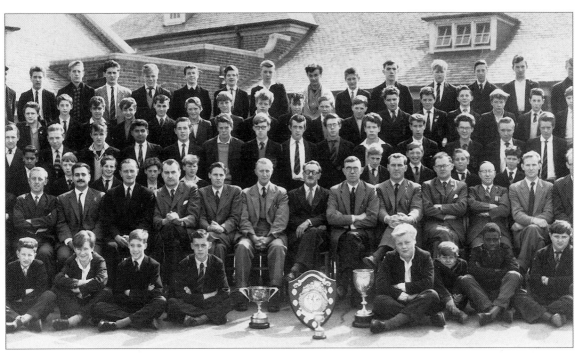

Pupils and staff from George Salter Secondary Boys School, *c.* 1962. Back row, left to right: -?-, -?-, ? Groom, David Knowles, Ron Evans, Michael Blanky, Alan Hill, Robert Stevenson, Alan Foster. Among the fifth row: Geoff Dicken, John Hall, John Harvey, ? Worker, John McGough. Fourth row: -?-, John Spooner, Keith Fletcher, Herman Patel, David Malborn, David Dixon, Frank Woodbine, Philip Evans, Alan Long, Lawrence Farley, Robert Lewis, ? Wild, Brian Holmes, Michael Southall, -?-. Second row: ? Holyhead, Albert Bidjikian, Les Oldhams, ? Clarke, 'Smiler' Smith, Edgar Bloor, Reg Turley, Jim Gardner, Jim Stevens, ? Green, ? Leek, ? Thomas, ? Edwards. (*David Malborn*)

George Salter School FC first XI, 1960/1 season. Back row, left to right: John Garbett, Jimmy Fox, John Howard, Jimmy Gittins, Brian Walford, David Bishop, David Pearsall. Front row: John Baker, Roy Geddes, Tony Brierley, Alan Doggett, Geoff Roper. (*Alan Doggett*)

'Pongo' Rapson's class 3M at George Salter Secondary Modern Girls School, *c.* 1956. Back row, left to right: Pat Garratt, Pat Sheldon, Sharon Carter, Gillian Marsdon, Christine Lawley, Valerie Stokes. Third row: Valerie Knowles, Barbara Whitehouse, Pat Willetts, Pat Bytheway, Virginia Whale, Joyce Colley, Pat ?, -?-, Pauline Nock, Desanka Phillips, Pat ?, -?-. Second row: Jean Holmes, Lillian Shaw, Pauline Simms, -?-, Jenny Evans, Valerie ?, Gillian ?, Barbara Clee, Margaret Johnson. Front row: Roseanne Sands, -?-, -?-, -?-, Joyce ?, Sylvia ?, Pat ?. (*Jennifer Edwards*)

George Salter School FC, *c.* 1955. Back row, left to right; Tom Hughes, Terry Nock, Jim Stevens, Donald Clements, Wilf Stokes, -?-. Front row: Roy Harris, Sid Cartwright, Keith Handley, Reg Turley (headmaster), Billy Harris, Michael Kellas, Brian Aston. (*Terry Nock*)

'The Willow Pattern Plate' presented by pupils of Fisher Street School, Great Bridge, during their 1958 concert party. Back row, left to right: Michael Darby, -?-, Josephine Reynolds. Third row: -?-, Robert Hann, -?-, -?-. Second row: -?-, John Hunt, Linda Sergeant, Susan Fletcher. (*Bertha Griffiths*)

The teaching staff of Fisher Street School, Great Bridge, autumn 1966. Back row, left to right: Norman Riley, Molly Boughton, Kate Harris, David Edwards, Chris Lloyd, Tom Shaw (lollipop man). Front row: Rita Hallard, Doreen Eden, Monica Richards (headmistress), Bertha Griffiths, Joyce Horton.
(*Monica Richards*)

Mrs Lily Weaver's top class at Fisher Street School working hard making festive party hats, Christmas 1953. Left side desks: Valerie Burns, Maureen Bailey, Josie Kennett, John Fereday. Right side desks: Pat Tillison, Peter Homer, Linda Whitehouse. The headmistress at the time was Miss Lucy Ellen Swinnerton. (*Lily Weaver*)

Fisher Street School FC, Great Bridge, 1958/9 season. Back row, left to right. Martin Whitehouse, Alan Worley, David Marsden, Keith Witton, Frank Wootton, John Worley, Tony Bishop, John Aston, Ray Cooper. Front row: Terry Johnson, Alan Beckett, David Cartwright, Michael Parry, Barry Jinks. (*Monica Richards*)

Pupils performing a Hawaiian dance during a concert held at Fisher Street School, Great Bridge, 1959. Left to right: Pauline Sheldon, Margaret Stott, Wendy Blakemore, Susan Homer, Sanchia Duggan, Mary Saxon. (*Monica Richards*)

Members of the concert party held in 1959 at Fisher Street School, Great Bridge. Back row, left to right: Keith Witton, John Worley, John Aston, David Marsden, Barry Salt, Brian Reed, Tony Bishop, Alan Beckett. Front row: Jimmy Bagley, Terry Hann, Michael Parry, Michael Darby, Graham Pearson, Terry Johnson, Gordon Richards, David Dugmore. (*Monica Richards*)

Greets Green School swimming team, winners of the inter-schools trophy, 1964. Teacher, Mercy Summerton, (top left), was at Dudley Training College from 1931 until 1933 before joining Joseph Edward Cox School at Friar Park as a junior teacher in 1934. In August 1936 she was forced to give up this position as a result of her marriage to Thomas (top right) because married women were not allowed to have teaching positions in those days. However, in 1946 she returned to teaching on a temporary contract at Greets Green School, which continued until the school closed in 1972. After moving to Newtown Infants and Primary School for a short while, she finally retired in July 1973. Headmaster, Thomas Summerton, began his teaching career at Cronehills Selective Central School in 1932 and then moving the same year to Golds Hill. A short spell at Bratt Street School followed in 1933 before securing an appointment at Greets Green, becoming headmaster there in 1948. In between this he also served in the Royal Artillery from 1940 until 1945. He retired from the teaching profession in 1971. Back row, left to right: Mercy Summerton, Gary Stokes, Graham Perry, Stewart Reynolds, Thomas George Summerton. Middle row, centre: Neil Ross. (*Stewart Reynolds*)

Greets Green School FC, 1955/6 season. Back row, left to right: Alf Darby, Thomas G. Summerton, Geraint Williams. Third row: Michael Grainger, Ernie Hughes, Colin Markham, Donald Insley, Sam Tudor, John Dixon, Gerald Durrant. Second row: Gilbert Heath, Percy Wilson, Selwyn Vale, John Jacks, Michael Davies. Front row: Ray Taft. (*Ernie Hughes*)

Guns Lane Junior and Infants School, class 1 mixed infants, 1932. The teacher on the left was Miss Gladys Butler, later to become Mrs Gladys Welsh. Pupils include, back row: Sybil Whitehouse, Bernard Fieldhouse. Third row: Florrie Steen, Tommy Oakley, Raymond Jukes. Second row: Harry Lowe. Front row: Mary Stocking, Alfie Collins, Vera Burns, Gladys Hill. Also in the picture: Richard Poxon, Ike Plant, Fred Terrett, Ida Mills, Ernie Wheatley, Joey White. (*Gladys Welsh*)

Hamstead Junior and Infants School, form 3 infants, *c.* 1953. Among the front row: Christine Onions (Teacher), Ken Davis, David Powell, Alan Holliday, Dorothy Leedham. Third row: Peter Steggall, Andrea Fitzpatrick, Rita Baker. Second row: Glynis Coles, Kathleen Hollier, Sally Fox, Laurence Turner, Diane Worthy, Susan Brady. Front row: Margaret Mutton, Susan Danks. (*Edith Davies*)

All Saints' Junior School camp at Plas-Gwynant, 1959. Third row, left to right: Ken Bissell, Frances Barraclough, Mary Bissell, ? Barraclough (Headmistress), Roger Fairweather. Front row: -?-, -?-, Christopher Bissell, -?-, Kathryn Bissell, -?-, -?-, -?-. (*Ken Bissell*)

Hamstead Junior and Infants School, *c.* 1956. Back row, left to right: Reg Jones (headmaster), Roy Furnival, Robert Pegg, -?-, Philip Simmonds, Ken Davies, Peter Steggall, Alan Holliday, Michael Flello, Vaughan Davies, Robert Tooth, David Powell, -?-, Harry Collett. Third row: ? Weaver, Peter Knowles, Pauline Wedgebury, -?-, Delia Dennis, -?-, Annette Landells, -?-, -?-, -?-, Andrea Fitzpatrick, Christine Richards, Kathleen Hollier, Rita Baker, Stephanie Davies, -?-, Margaret Wearing. Second row: -?-, Susan Brady, -?-, -?-, Diane Worthy, -?-, Marlene Bull, Glynis Coles, Lynn Williams, Diane Partridge, Sally Fox, -?-. (*Edith Davies*)

Beeches Road Junior and Infants School pageant, *c.* 1949. Evelyn Matthews is fourth from the left, back row, while Diane Hickman is second from the right. First from the right, front row is Valerie Haynes. (*Evelyn Gough*)

Holy Trinity Junior School class, *c.* 1947. Back row, left to right: Tom Crisp (Headmaster), Michael Round, Chris Smith, Peter Sheldon, George Nash, -?-, Ray Jenkins, Richard Parish, Harold Baker, David Firkin, Jeff Farmer, -?-, Alfred Bunn, Ron Rudge, -?-, Sid Evans. Middle row: John Theatre, Janet Howman, Jillian Wall, Carol Stokes, Sheila Oakley, Annette Powell, Jean Smith, Gwen Timmins, Freda Forrest, Betty Mullett, Jean Gilbert, Joan Shakespear, -?-. Front row: Janet Masters, Gwen Horton, Irene Butwell, Mavis Fewtrell, -?-, Valerie Judge, -?-, Jean Horton, Janet Williams, Pat Bartram, -?-, Janet Hodgetts, -?-, Sheila Mountford. (*Iris Reynolds*)

Charlemont Junior School, form 4A, *c.* 1951. Back row, left to right: Linda Lees, Vera Nicholson, Linda Lewis, Pauline Pearsall, Barbara Wilcox, Jillian Stanley, Ken Bissell, Jacqueline Howell, Jean Parker, Janet Cadman, Pauline Tanner, Edith Nock, Margaret Pritchard. Third row: Brian Cope, David Hinson, Hazel Stone, Veronica Dilworth, Betty Hale, Sylvia Altree, -?-, Ann Carless, Mavis James, Robert Houghton, Philip Newman, Norman Horton. Second row: Patrick Mason, Michael Stanton, Frank Griffiths, Margaret Yates, Pat Jones, Barbara Whiles, Janice Turley, Sylvia Greenaway, Maureen Carimes, Trevor Atterbury, Colin MacManus, Brian Markham. (*Ken Bissell*)

Charlemont Junior School at Shenstone Lodge camp, 1951. Back row, left to right: Joan Banks, Pam Beasley -?-, Pauline Pearsall, Janet Satterthwaite, Ken Bissell, Dorothy Pritchard, Valerie Gorton, Mary Bissell, Linda Lewis, -?-. Middle row: Jill ?, Janet Cadman, Gillian Bunn, Margaret Pritchard, Jillian Standley, Ann Carless, -?- Janet Withers. Front row: Hazel Stone, ? Stone, ? Hale, Betty Hale, Veronica Dilworth, Margaret Yates, Pat Page, Josie Johnson, Evelyn Coker. (*Mary Bissell*)

West Bromwich Grammar School FC, 1952/3 season. Back row, left to right: Philip 'Ted' Ray, Clem Cotterill, Ken Corbett, Tom Hanley, John Turner, ? Todd. Front row: John Flanagan, Chris Thayne, -?-, Lawrence Lees, -?-, Howard Baker, Colin Johnson. (*Tom Handley*)

West Bromwich Municipal Secondary School, form 1C, May 1933. Back row, left to right: Wilfred Edwards, Peter Hunter, Stanley Wilkins, Raymond Marsh, Ronald Martin, Barry Hipkiss, Glyndor Savory, Tommy Turner, Dennis Bridgewater. Fourth row: Euphram Hinton, Doris Allen, Kitty Palmer, Gladys Baker, Kathleen Akehurst, Vera Turner, Joan Clark, Molly Higgins. Third row: Doris Whitehouse, Peggy Woodward, Marjorie Jones, Joan Turner, Bertha Walwynn, Joyce Pollard, Dorothy Llewellyn, Betty Brand, Gladys Richards, Lily Billingham. Second row: Dennis Wilkins, William Knight, Maurice Turner, Peter Brown, Dennis Longbottom, Robert Knowles. Front row: Maurice Piket, Tom Silk, Tom Phipps. (*Stan Wilkins*)

West Bromwich Grammar School, first XI cricket team, *c.* 1952. Back row, left to right: Roy Griffiths, S. Smalley, John Turner, F. Perry, Clem Cotterill, Philip 'Ted' Ray. Front row: Maurice Payne, Tom Handley, Colin Osborne, Eric Patterson, Eric Worley, Alan MacKenzie, Maurice Poulton. (*Tom Handley*)

West Bromwich Grammar School, form 2L, *c.* 1939. Back row: left to right: Ted Culwick, George Johns, Brian Wood, Alan Patrick, Stan Edwards, Ken Bissell, John Hill, Bill Stanfield, Alan Webster. Third row: ? Hall, Joyce Crump, Barbara Green, Joy ?, Kathleen Bridge, Eileen ?, Nancy Walker, Irene Howes, Mary Cooksey, Tony Cooper. Second row: Marion Williams, Masie Newey, Iris Vanes, Jean Cooper, Joseph Austin, Muriel Turner, Mary Robinson, Valerie Pegg, Alison Barlow. Front row: Raymond Wood, Alan Garrett, Eric Williams, Eric Carpenter, Alan Brookes, Frank Bryant. (*Iris Gill*)

West Bromwich Municipal Secondary School, summer 1936. Back row, third from right: Ken Brookes. Third row, left to right: John Potter, Doreen Sower, Ursula Parry, Eileen Jones, Mary Williams, -?-, Irene Rochester, Laura Mantle, -?-, -?-. Second row: Joan Baggott, Joanna Manley, Maisie Cole, Monsieur Bertrand, Edith Isaacs, Mary Longhurst, Audrey Leadbeater, Mary Hawkes, -?-. Front row: -?-, -?-, -?-, -?-, Eric Painter, Brian Thomas. (*Joan Oldhams*)

West Bromwich Municipal Secondary School, form 4L, 1936. Back row, left to right: John Orchard, Albert Evans, Raymond Marsh, Barry Hipkiss, Eddie Pickett, Michael Howell, Dennis Rhodes, ? Law. Middle row: Robert Bowles, Stan Wilkins, Betty Russell, Edna Davies, Edith Smith, Maurice Larner, Glyndor Savory, Norman Riley. Front row: Stella Palfreyman, Audrey Whiteman, Dorothy Stringer, Jean Ault, John 'Pat' Carroll, Dorothy Llewellyn, Doris Whitehouse, Dorothy Grice, Doreen Danter. (*Stan Wilkins*)

Pupils of Joseph Edward Cox School, Friar Park (West Bromwich), *c.* 1952. Back row, left to right: -?-, Jim Riley, -?-, -?-, Tony Ore, John Sheppard, Alan Hinton, -?-, Doug Smith, Malcolm Tromans, Brian Ike. Third row: Michael West, Geoffrey Johnson, Peter Atterbury, Pat Edgerton, -?-, -?-, -?-, -?-, Harold Freeth, Geoffrey Hunt. Among the second row: Dorothy Hawkes, Ivy Attwell (teacher), June Clive. Front row: -?-, George Oliver, Raymond Glendenning, Fred Owen, -?-. (*John Sheppard*)

Cronehills Selective Central School, form 1A, 1931. Back row, left to right: Phylis Warrender, Freda ?, Dorothy Shakespeare, Dorothy Morgan, -?-, Dorothy Summerfield, Edna Povey, Freda ?, Florrie Tucker Fourth row: Joan Butler, -?-, Olive ?, Doreen ?, -?-, -?-, Olive Butler, ? Hickman, ? Harris, -?-, -?-. Third row: Ivy Danks, Ella Plant, Joan Finch, Nora Freeman, Miss Williams, Brenda Sergeant, Barbara Jones, -?-, -?-, -?-. Second row: Alice Pritchard, -?-, -?-, Mary Davies, Joan Passfield. (*Anita Warner*)

Lyng Junior School, *c.* 1950. Back row, left to right: Alan Whitehouse, Trevor Bevan, Tommy Furnival, Colin Lucock, Tony Morley, Tony Harris, John Bailey, David Jones, Tony Kendrick, David James, Bob Taylor, Brian Dearn, Michael Felton, Miss Lee. Middle row: Brian Cartwright, Ray Bibb, Trevor Morris, Keith Vincent, Alan Marshall, Ray Corbett, John Wyatt, Trevor Coles, Michael Reynolds, Billy Harris, Brian Richards, Alan Smith, Bernard Holt, Pat Smith. Front row: Frank Baker, Michael Woodfield, Eddie Harris, Bob Cooper, Harry Bates, Malcolm Dodson, Brian Hadley, Sam Welborn, Teddy Roden, Eddie Stone, Alan Davies, Desmond Stanton, Billy Turner. (*Brian Richards*)

Spon Lane Secondary Modern School teaching staff, *c.* 1952. Back row, left to right: -?-, 'T Square' Dutton, 'Eric' Amery, -?-, Don 'Dan' Derbyshire, Derek 'Dougie' Oldhams, -?-, Ted Turton, Dickie Law. Front row: John 'Pansie' Potter, Richard 'Dickie' Lowe, Gerry 'Big Daddy' Edwards, Francis 'Charlie' Walton, Reg 'Happy' Hutton, -?-, Jasper Hill. (*Joan Oldhams*)

Lyng School FC, 1949/50 season. Back row, left to right: ? Hodgkinson, ? Gutteridge, Peter Woodward Third row: Brian Eaton, Graham Peplow, John Bevan, Harry Matty, Ken Hadley, Terry Mason. Second row Paul Scholfield, John Garland, Brian Collett, Alan Cartwright, Ron Bevan. Front row: Brian Cartwright Colin Lucock. (*Brian Collett*)

Lyng School FC, 1950/1 season. Back row, left to right: Peter Powell, Tony Morley, Alan Marshall, Ray Corbett, Colin Lucock, Michael Woodfield. Middle row: Sid Cartwright, Alan James, Peter Woodward, Brian Cartwright, Geoff Green. Front row: Eddie Stone, David Jones, David Read. (*Eddie Stone*)

Harvills Hawthorn School FC, *c.* 1979. Back row, left to right: Mike Smith, Tony Arnold, ? Fullwood, ? Butler, Malcolm Lloyd, Ian Shiels, Mark Wright. Front row: Ken Bissell, Kevin Jackson, Brett Burgess, Malcolm Wright, Alan Cox, Ken Homer, Ian Wright. (*Ken Bissell*)

Hall Green Junior and Infants School, 1979. Back row, left to right: Katherine Knowles, Melanie Shinton, Steven Wood, Rachel Hoult, Fiona Legister, Stephanie Parks, Joanne Allen, Anthony Carby, Michelle Phillips, Angela Walker, Carla Oliver, Donna Moore, Graham Stocking. Fourth row: Jason Southall, Michelle Hooper, Claire ?, Louise Skidmore, Claire Stocking, Kerry Roberts, Claire Melia, Dean Hughes, Lee Eccles. Third row: Brenda Wiseman, Brett Dicks, Patrick Walton, Tony Latham, Lisa Russell, Andrew Jarvis, Christopher Brookes, Sanjiv Paul, Elsie Cartwright. Second row: Richard Tromans, Michael Bateman, Craig Foster, Lisa Garmston, Christopher Monk, -?-. Front row: Claire Lloyd, Jason Rowley, Lisa Farmer, Debbie Bryceland, Stephen Slade, Scott Wills, Joanne Tycer, Joanne Higgs. (*Elsie Cartwright*)

ACKNOWLEDGEMENTS

I wish to thank the many friends who loaned me photographs and without whose help this compilation would not have been possible. All the contributors' names have been acknowledged at the end of each caption. My thanks also go to the following people for their support, including all those who provided me with additional information: Doris Abbotts, Annie Ball, Beryl Barnes, Jim Barnfield, John Bayliss, Ken and Mary Bissell, Ian Bott, Chris Brown, Keith Cherrington, Sam Chiles, Violet and Joshua Churchman, Joyce Cooper, Fred Dell, Jackie Evans, Bob Franks, Ann George, Iris Gill, Reg Hannington, Keith Hodgkins, Ken Hodgkisson, Kathleen Homeshaw, Joan and Joseph Howes, Bill Inkson, Ian Marks, Tony Matthews, Andrew Maxam, Margaret Morgan, Vera Morris, Anthony Page, Robin Pearson, Kathleen Powell, Mary Powell, Lily Phillips, Alan Price, Joan Pymm, Iris Reynolds, Ken Rock, Jim and Mary Rose, Ivy Round-Hancock, Dorothy Smith, Eddie Stone, Eric Stott, Mercy Summerton, Ann Taylor, Beattie Thompson, Brian Whitehouse, Sheila Whitehouse, Ned Williams, David Wilson, Ted Woodward.

I am also grateful to: *Birmingham Post & Mail*, Crown Cards, Custom Printing, Sidney Darby & Son Ltd., West Bromwich Library, Walsall Local History Centre.

Thanks also to Rob Davies and Jo Walker of the *Wolverhampton Express & Star*.

Once again many thanks to Dr Carl Chinn MBE for his support and encouragement.

My special thanks to *Dawn Davey* for typing the manuscript.

Finally to my wife Beryl for her patience and understanding.

Dr Carl Chinn MBE addressing an audience of around 400 people in support of the launch by Terry Price of his first book, at Wesley Church, West Bromwich, on Saturday 30 September 2000. (*Nigel Hazelwood*)